The 7 Stages of Grief
A Practical Workbook for Transformation

EMBRACE

"While evoking deep-seated emotions, my writings aim to transcend readers along a shared journey of refined frequencies of illumination." —Michele Bell

M.C. BELL
THE GRIEF WARRIOR®

Honoring the Journey
of Unconditional Love

A tribute to those who've known grief's face.
In the Healing it Forward Journey's embrace,
They move with courage at their own pace.

In the story of life, they've taken a dare,
To love deeply, to truly care.
For they understand it's not a solitary fight,
Grief's touch is universal, a shared plight.

In the canvas of existence, painted gray,
They've known loss, in its shadowed way.
A reminder, as we journey each day,
Love's depths may fade, but in our hearts,
the memories will forever st fo

Love with a fierceness, both deep and rare,
In their hearts, the pain they bear and share.
Through farewells and tears, they dare,
To love fully, a bond beyond compare.

"We Are Not Alone," their voices proclaim,
In unity, they kindle hope's gentle flame.
This book reminds us that life's not the same,
With their wisdom, we're part of love's grand game.

So let's honor those who've paid the cost,
In their stories, love is never lost.
In the tapestry of existence, they emboss.
Healing It Forward, is a tale worth the exhaust.

M. C. BELL

The EMBRACE Journey
Transform Grief and Discover Inner *Strength*

Welcome, Warriors, to the extraordinary dimension of the 7 Stages of Grief Workbook Journal. I will guide you through a miraculous and empowering passage, unveiling the hidden treasures amidst the labyrinth of trauma and loss.

This course was born from my authentic desire to *heal it forward* in the grief community, ignited by theta meditation and a deep desire to manifest growth and healing through my writings. Drawing upon my intuitive theta-visions, I have created the EMBRACE framework — a radiant constellation of seven stages illuminating our transformative expedition in the wake of adversity.

In contrast to conventional approaches that merely skim the surface of emotions within the limited confines of the five stages of grief, I sensed the dire need for a holistic and transformative tapestry. The 7 stages of grief, meticulously crafted through my Healing it Forward modalities used in my 1:1 sacred retreats, transcend the ephemeral realm of emotions, ushering us into a realm where storytelling, the sacred utterance of our beloved's name, and the cultivation of gratitude mingle, guiding us through each challenging obstacle that graces our path.

Within this cherished community of kindred souls, we will unite, bound by a shared mission to collaborate, share our truth, and breathe life into one another's spirits—a sacred alchemy that fosters a radiant cascade of healing and metamorphosis. The modalities unveiled in the EMBRACE workbook journal's resplendent pages revolutionized how we navigate our sacred inner landscape, transforming the lives of those who have an unwavering longing to embrace the transformative work ahead.

As an extraordinary boon, I invite you to journey beside me as a Certified Grief Wellness Warrior, armed with the profound and purposeful modalities needed to extend a gentle hand to those ensnared in the clutches of their grief. By immersing yourself in these transformative practices and obtaining certification, you shall illuminate the path for others in their darkest moments, serving as a beacon of light and hope amidst the unfathomable abyss.

With deepest gratitude and genuine admiration, I extend my heartfelt appreciation to you for summoning the courage to embark upon the sacred journey of the EMBRACE workbook journal course. I assure you, Warriors, that this decision shall cascade with blessings and profoundly resonate. Together, let us traverse the infinite depths of grief, unlocking the wellspring of our inner fortitude and embarking upon a journey that transcends healing alone—a voyage brimming with purpose, renewal, and the willful power of the human spirit.

Prepare yourself for the transformational power of the 7 Stages of Grief Workbook Journal.

Let our extraordinary odyssey begin.

The Grief Warrior

Table of Contents

Forward 03

From My Heart to Yours 05

Prolonged Grief Disorder Unveiled 06

Unveiling the Truth: The Evolution 07

Why Prolonged Grief Disorder is Facing So Much Criticism 08

Unlock the Profound Power of Healing with EMBRACE 10

EMBRACE: The 7 Stages of Grief Alignment 12

If You're Ready To Turn Your Pain Into Fuel 14

Pivot with Purpose 15

I Had Two Choices: Retreat Or Renew 16

Our Joyful Ending: Pain Meets Healing 17

How To Sit with Your Grief 18

Are You Living a Life of Denial? 21

The Guiding Light of Embrace: Nurturing Those in Grief 22

The Healing Dance of Grief Nurturing the Spirit within 23

Why Do Some People Run When I EMBRACE My Sadness? 24

The Whispers of Compassion 25

The Unseen Language of Sorrow? Embracing Understanding 26

Unveiling the Art of Respecting Grief 28

Bottom Line 29

Does EMBRACE Speak to You? 31

Your inner spiritual warrior! 36

FOREWARD

My name is Cristal Sampson, and I work in mental health and psychiatry as a nurse practitioner in Connecticut and New York, specializing in traumatic stress and mood disorders. I am also a woman who experienced an early-term spontaneous miscarriage that burned a hole in my depths I had previously not known existed. The revelation of this new depth of unconditional Love, coupled with my baby's teeny heart-stopping, left me hollow.

Even in my subsequent pregnancy the following year, I still felt empty of the unfulfillable desire for the baby back that I had lost in this life. The emptiness was filled with sadness, anxiety, and disappointment from troubled family dynamics – a family unaware of my loss and grief.

Someone like me in my expertise is never immune to the heartaches of the human experience, like loss of love and life. I recognized the potential to be an emotionally-absent mother to my unborn baby, which was all but set in stone at the time – and the thought terrified me. I am grateful to have known that I owed my baby and myself the chance to heal. In my research, I found Michele, The Grief Warrior.

As a health professional and a mental health professional, I tend to be incredibly picky about whom I receive services from and what services I seek. At this period in my life and for this circumstance, I did not seek "traditional" mental health counseling. At the time, I could not face modern therapy's issues. I saw the potential for the more traditional route as most helpful later in my healing.

What Michele offered touched the core, breadth, and depth of my hurting, going deep into the spiritual, mental, emotional, and energetic spaces of my being, body, and surroundings through a one-on-one retreat. I've experienced nothing like it since, so I am moved that you are here reading the 7 Stages of Grief. Your experience will change you with Michele's intentional energy through her books.

FOREWARD

EMBRACE: The 7 Stages of Grief Alignment is created for every griefer; everyone feeling unqualified for and overwhelmed by the legal proceedings of loss of life; for those of us who are suffering alone because we can't bring ourselves to speak our emotional pain out loud to someone just yet or because you are keeping the pending end-of-life secret at the request of your loved one; for everyone cycling between the pain of anticipating a loss of precious life to needing to "hold it together" for your "normal" life and responsibilities to becoming angry and resentful back to pain again; and for every caregiver who needs care.

My favorite part about Michele's 7 Stages of Grief is how she provides practical hope, by which I mean she has found the natural places where hope lives, bringing those places to light in this book. Michele is masterful at navigating the abundance of resources available to the caregiver and leads you to the path of help that is pragmatic and accessible. Michele is intimately aware of the caregiver's life because she gracefully helped her teenage son Nicky transition and was surrounded by much love.

My work with Michele has caused a seismic shift in my perspective and has improved my relationships with myself, my family, and the people who meet me. I am moved with infinite gratitude at the positive and priceless impact my work with Michele has had on my experience of motherhood and the beautiful relationship my daughter and I get to have. Now, I enjoy expanding my connection as she has become a selfless friend and true mentor.

I invite you to let this book change you for the better. Let this book support you and be there for you daily, especially when needed. Let this book be your guide. I want to leave you with this: Everything Michele has done since Nicky's return to Source has been a love letter to Nicky and a tribute to the permanent imprint of love and purpose he left with her. Ultimately, Michele hopes you may find your purpose and let it propel you through the rest of your precious life.

Cristal Sampoon

FROM MY HEART
to yours...

Alignment in the face of loss is the only option. When we open ourselves to the possibilities presented to us, we find this harmony: in the strength of our words, in the peace of our meditations, in the gift of our presence, in the renewal of our bodies, in the stirring of our spirits, in the depth of our relationships, and in the nourishment we give ourselves.

The path to recovery is a beautiful tapestry that offers the opportunity for personal development and the forging of inner fortitude. We will brave new territory together, learn new things, and grow as people. I will be your guide and source of solace throughout our journey together. Get ready to reclaim your life with renewed confidence as you learn to swiftly navigate life's complications and unleash your remarkable inner potential.

There is nothing scary or complicated about this course since I will be there to guide you through every one of the steps. Let's take off on a journey into the unknown, where the payoff to SELF could be infinite.

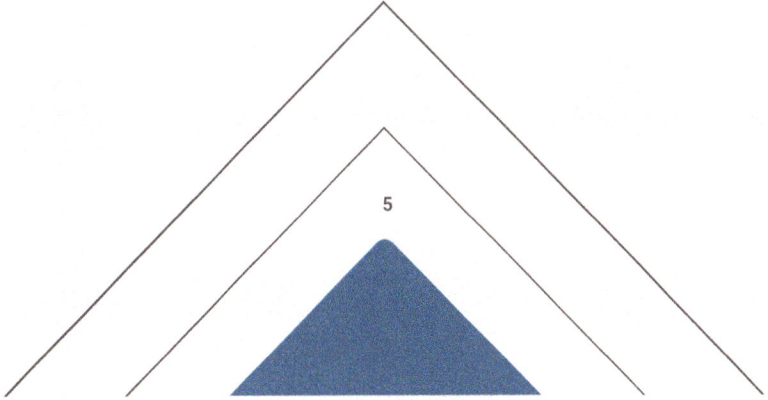

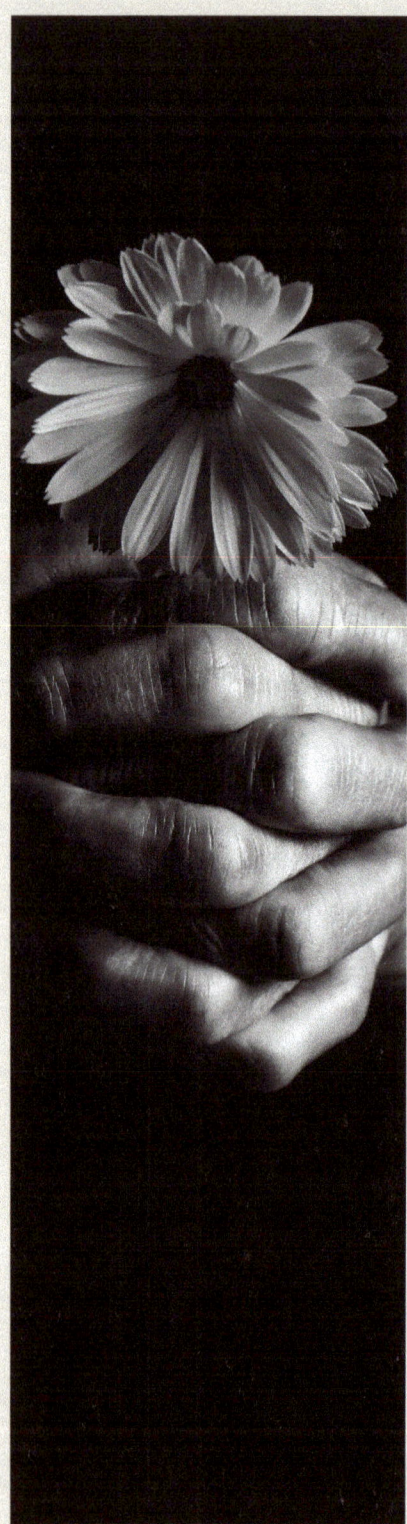

PROLONGED GRIEF DISORDER
Unveiled
as total B.S

Shattering the Illusion: Liberating Ourselves from the Constraints of the "5 Stages of Grief"

Adhering to established norms is a delusion, a fallacy we must quickly let go of when dealing with extended grief disorder. The "5 Stages of Bereavement" model developed by psychologists has been widely disseminated for too long, permeating every aspect of grief counseling and education.

Unfortunately, the constant push to conform to a set and narrow path of grieving has led me and countless other seekers within the grief community to feel disillusioned.

I beg you to disregard this erroneous advice immediately. The core meaning of our name, "EMBRACE," contains the whole truth. The concept of "Prolonged Grief Disorder" is 100% bogus.

The "5 Stages of Grief" concept originated from an unsupported theory meant to characterize the reaction of people who had been given fatal diagnoses rather than those who were navigating the maze of loss and sorrow. Here we have two utterly dissimilar yet actual experiences, each of which calls for special attention and comprehension.

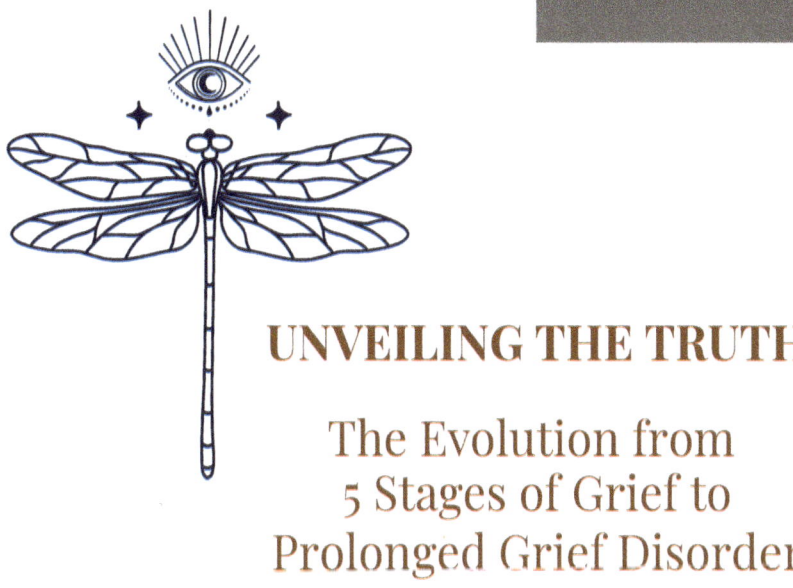

UNVEILING THE TRUTH

The Evolution from 5 Stages of Grief to Prolonged Grief Disorder

In March 2022, a new grief-related disorder was officially adopted into mainstream mental health diagnosis nomenclature. Seeing how the clinical world has further shamed the sacred grieving world is disheartening. DSM-5's trauma and stress-related category have a new label: Prolonged Grief Disorder, created deliberately to define what grief should and should not look like.

But first, let's take a moment to think. What exactly is this thing called "Prolonged Grief Disorder"? Claiming a year for adults and a paltry six months for children is an arrogant attempt to restrict the complex fabric of grief inside the confines of time. According to the American Psychological Association, persons who carry this label are assumed to exhibit the following symptoms even after the diagnostic window has closed:

- The crushing weight of grief pressed down on every aspect of their being.
- An unending fixation on sorrow as memories of the lost reverberate ceaselessly.
- A mental panorama obscured by agony or the unsettling absence of feeling.
- They engage in a delicate dance of denial and avoidance as they try to face their loved one's death.
- Dissonance and disconnection can develop when one feels different from the social norm.
- Every breath is filled with the haunting repercussions of despair and isolation.

We stand at the intersection of societal, cultural, and religious expectations, where the mere fulfillment of established criteria has become pivotal in making a prognosis. Understandably, when engulfed by the darkness of losing a loved one, such clinical classifications may not bring the peace and comprehension one wants.

To promote genuine healing, we need to permit ourselves to explore our inner emotional landscape freely.

Let us stand up as one in our resolve to overcome this stereotype's obstacles. Let us regain our freedom from societal norms to grieve and heal as we see fit.

We will overcome obstacles as a group and EMBRACE the journey of getting to the heart of our pain and reclaiming our ways forward in healing.

WHY PROLONGED GRIEF DISORDER
is Facing So Much Criticism

There is no moral compass in the arena of mourning.

Grief isn't reducible to a single feeling but incorporates many of them. It weaves a complex and ever-changing mosaic of emotions, including sadness, rage, anguish, loneliness, reverence, connection, and perplexity.

It's a shared adventure that everyone does on their terms.

Grief is complex and multifaceted: No two souls mourn alike, for no two losses are identical. Attempts to confine the grieving process within cookie-cutter stages, rigid criteria, and prescribed timelines propagate the fallacy of a right or wrong way to grieve.

Grief, in its essence, is a natural phenomenon—

A sacred dance that unfolds within the depths of our being. It is a deeply personal and profound experience, far from being a pathological problem to be solved.

A child's heart carries the imprint of a parent's absence for months or years. Similarly, a parent's longing for a child, partner, or loved one transcends all notions of time. The ache, the longing, lives in the very essence of our human nature.

Grief is an enigmatic path; Grief isn't linear.—

If we were to create a line graph of our grief journeys, it would be surprising for scientists to discover no discernible pattern.

Within the ebb and flow of our grief, we encounter good and bad days interwoven in a twisted dance.

Embracing this is how we move with our grief. Labeling and attempting to confine it only breeds resistance. Progress lies *not* in imposing a specific timeline but in surrendering to the ever-changing flow of our grief and learning to move on with acceptance and dignity.

Grief isn't inherently harmful.

Grief is evidence of love lost.

It serves as a poignant symbol of our love, our desire to cherish and remember those individuals and relationships that hold deep significance in our lives.

It's instinctively human: both beautiful and painful. By labeling grief as a problem in this sacred space, By labeling grief as a problem to solve, we carry it. By leaning into our pain, we *move with* it.

Grief looms of isolation. Support becomes our lifeline.

Grief defies measurement, transcending the confines of milestones as the 5 Stages of Grief imply. It is an ever-evolving journey, an ongoing experience. Pathologizing and diagnosing grief makes it feel abnormal. In reality, it represents so much of the human experience.

Diagnoses can empower us by illuminating how our minds or bodies function differently and offering solutions. However, diagnosing grief only deepens the shame, loneliness, and isolation. No one should feel wrong for grieving beyond a specific date.

We need grief support, not grief diagnosis. By creating space for its expression, allowing its capacity to unfold without restraint.

Unlock the Profound Power of Healing with EMBRACE
The 7 Stages of Grief Alignment

Are you prepared to immerse yourself on a journey of healing and self-discovery?

Step into a sphere of authenticity, truth, and love as you immerse yourself in the unparalleled wisdom and guidance offered in the transformative EMBRACE course. This course goes beyond the ordinary, offering a depth of healing that will leave an indelible impact.

What sets EMBRACE apart? It emerges from the heart of an expert grief practitioner, infused with the spirit of authenticity and infused by a genuine desire to empower and support individuals on their unique healing journeys.

EMBRACE offers a transformative approach that transcends traditional teachings.

Through this meticulously crafted course, you will unlock the tools and techniques to navigate the depths of grief, embracing healing and growth. The 7 Stages of Grief Alignment workbook becomes your trusted companion, providing compassionate guidance through each stage. It empowers you to honor your journey, embrace your emotions, and pave the way for a purposeful shift.

However, EMBRACE's path forward still needs to be completed. Those interested in learning more and becoming certified "Healing it Forward" practitioners will find that this course provides a beautiful opportunity to do just that. As a trained professional, you will be honored to assist others on their journey to wholeness and personal development.

The EMBRACE program is an astonishing journey of self-discovery and empowerment, not simply another healing class. It encourages you to look within, where you'll find the key to your inner wisdom and the key to your recovery. Along the journey, you'll be surrounded and transformed by a community of like-minded spirits who share your unyielding dedication to growth and give support and encouragement.

Are you prepared to take your life's most incredible life-changing healing journey? Join us on this life-altering adventure, where our north stars are sincerity, honesty, and love. Learn the true meaning of pivoting with intent through your experience with EMBRACE. Your healing journey awaits, and we are here to walk alongside you every step of the way.

Are You Ready?

ALL RIGHT, GRIEF WARRIORS:

We're breaking up with the 5 Stages of Grief

Meet your new boo,
the 7 Stages of Grief Alignment!

The 7 Stages of Grief Alignment knows no order. They are not steps but continual pillars, symbols, and actions to make space for grief in your growth.

Words hold immense power, and we choose to transform our grief rather than diagnose it.

The Grief Warrior

EMBRACE

THE 7 STAGES OF GRIEF ALIGNMENT

01 EXPRESS
Let your emotions guide you and experience the joy and fulfillment of expressing your true self through journaling and artistic exploration.

02 MEDITATE
Embrace the power of sitting with your grief, opening your heart, and leaning into the serenity of the present moment, creating space for healing and growth.

03 BE PRESENT
Pause. Observe and relinquish the need for constant busyness, and tune into the depths of your feelings. Embrace the beauty, opportunity, and purpose in this moment.

04 REJUVENATE
Reignite your zest for life, nourish your soul, and elevate your vibrations through the transformative power of self-care. Rediscover what it means to feel truly alive.

05 AWAKEN
Awaken the part of you that's been hiding. Reclaiming lost joy, energy, and vibrance. Rediscover the essence of your true self, waiting to be revealed.

06 CONNECT
Grief can separate us from true ourselves, making us feel like trapped observers of our lives. Reconnect physically, mentally, and spiritually to find your center and regain a sense of control and profound connection.

07 EAT HEALTHY
Nourish your body with the fuel it craves for strength and vitality. Embrace the sensory delight of flavors, textures, and intuitive connection as your body receives each healthy bite.

What 'stage' speaks to you?

IF YOU'RE READY TO TURN YOUR PAIN INTO FUEL...

Your past can lead you to your purpose.

Your pain can become your fuel to embody and fulfill that purpose. It's time to heal the resilient spirit within you, the one who has overcome more than imagined possible.

Unclench your jaw. Let out a sigh of relief - and stop running. We can't change our pasts. e may not alter our pasts, but we can find peace in our history and shape our futures by nurturing our souls in the present moment.

Each of us possesses a unique narrative shaped by our experiences. While we may not always have control over the plot, we have the power to choose the underlying theme. Let us craft our stories around the essence of healing rather than being defined by pain.

Rise as a warrior, not just a survivor. I am here to guide you because I believe in your strength.

It's time to take hold of the reins and chart a path toward healing, love, and inner strength.

i believe in you.

> *Your past paves the path to purpose.*

🖊 **Grab a pen, and we'll embark on your new journey together.**

PIVOT *with* PURPOSE

My vocation is a sacred calling, where every word, line, and page is carefully crafted with intention and purpose. My vocation extends far beyond the conventional realms. It transcends the boundaries of traditional academia and ventures into the realm of energy and transcendence.

Having traversed the depths of deep trauma and loss, I intimately understand the weight of grief and despair. Yet, I alchemize that suffering into meaning through the art of writing, creating, and teaching. I am fueled by authentic and intentional love in every breath of my life.

It is not a love born out of obligation but a love that empowers and inspires, beckoning others to rise above their fears and embrace the limitless possibilities that lie within them.

To me, this is the very essence of sacredness.

Let this inspire you that, no matter your challenges, you can *Pivot with Purpose* and manifest life in alignment with your highest energy. As your Grief Warrior® mentor, I will guide you on a sacred transformation journey.

I HAD TWO CHOICES:
Retreat Or Renew

When my first-born son passed away, grief consumed me. I could have withdrawn from life, but a fire within me refused to give up. It was then that I realized grief is the expression of love. It's our mind and heart's way of grappling with loss. It requires embracing the unknown, for life itself is unpredictable, regardless of our beliefs.

In rediscovering the magic of life, I rekindled my commitment to live truly. The grief didn't vanish, but it became more manageable. I started noticing the small things that bring joy to life. Each day became an adventure filled with endless possibilities. With an open heart, I welcomed the uncertainties that came my way. While the aftermath of a loss can leave us feeling hopeless, the strength to persevere can lead to unexpected achievements. Withdrawing may seem tempting, but it only perpetuates a downward spiral. We can move forward and rediscover joy by renewing our commitment to purposeful living.

I crafted the 7 Stages of Grief Alignment to renew my commitment—a guide from eleven years of personal experience and introspection. My book, A Son's Gift, became a testament to living intentionally after unforeseen circumstances. This challenge navigates the unexpected tragedies that may befall us, particularly if we face intense grief for the first time. Each stage holds significance, and we must traverse them daily. It isn't always easy, but a life infused with meaning and purpose is worthwhile.

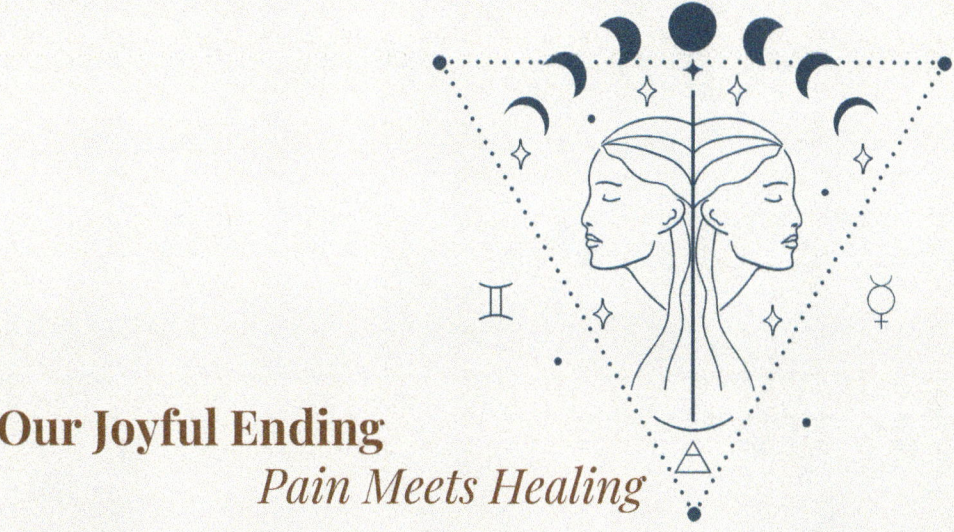

Our Joyful Ending
Pain Meets Healing

Once upon a time,

...in the whimsical land of Serenityville, a group of courageous warriors known as the Serene Seekers set forth on a remarkable quest—the Journey of Healing it Forward. Guided by the wise and enchanting fairy Seraphina, they discovered the secret power of acceptance. The goal was to align with the 7 Stages of Grief and release the mystical power inside.

The Serene Seekers set out on their journey full of bravery and love. As they wandered through enchanted forests and sparkling waterways, they experienced times of hardship. They didn't shy away since they knew the answer to their problems resided within themselves.

The Serene Seekers blazed a trail based on the ancient wisdom of the 7 Stages of Grief Alignment. Each phase—"Express," "Meditate," "Be Present," "Rejuvenate," "Awaken," "Connect," and "Eat Healthy"—held a vital piece of the puzzle to their recovery and development.

Under Seraphina's guidance, the Serene Seekers learned that pain was not their enemy but a teacher to be embraced. It became a part of their story, a testament to their courage and resilience. United in their journey, they supported one another, sharing stories and offering solace when needed. Their empathy and compassion wove a love web across Serenityville.

By embracing their pain, the Serene Seekers discovered the profound magic of healing it forward. They realized their healing could inspire and uplift others, spreading hope and resilience far and wide.

The Serene Seekers' journey through the 7 Stages of Grief Alignment showcased the power of acceptance and showed the world how beautiful it can be. Their travels exemplified the concept of "healing it forward," the idea that one person's kindness may positively impact others.

And so, the Serene Seekers continued their noble quest, fueled by determination and love. Together, they embarked on the Journey of Healing It Forward, embracing their pain, sharing their stories, and spreading seeds of healing throughout Serenityville and beyond.

This uplifting tale illustrates the power of facing our suffering and moving with "Healing it Forward."

HOW TO
Sit *with* Your Grief

ACKNOWLEDGE IT.

OWN IT.

EXPLORE IT.

THERE ARE 3 FUNDAMENTAL
STEPS TO EMBRACING YOUR GRIEF

FEEL *and* ACKNOWLEDGE IT

Feel - Dive into the Depths of Emotion In the first step. We will learn the art of feeling. Relax your body and mind by closing your eyes and taking a few slow, deep breaths. Don't oppose or judge the feelings you're experiencing.

Are you on the verge of purging, overwhelmed by a storm of pain, guilt, shame, betrayal, or envy?

In EMBRACE, you will understand the depth of your pain through emotional exploration. Embracing our feelings shows respect for the integrity of our experience and lays the foundation for healing.

To *acknowledge* is to embrace the power of acceptance with the courage to feel. It is easy to dismiss our grief, burying it beneath layers of denial or self-judgment. But this step teaches us to embrace our pain by acknowledging its presence. Let go of the urge to push your feelings aside or berate yourself for struggling. Instead, recognize that grief is a natural and valid experience. When you own your suffering, you allow yourself the time and perspective to determine what's causing it.

OWN YOUR FEELINGS
of Pain, Grieving, Loss

Understanding your feelings is the first step, but owning your pain is crucial. Grief is often associated with a side of ourselves that we prefer to ignore, so we dismiss it. However, pushing your emotions aside or criticizing yourself for struggling can worsen things. Instead, it's essential to accept your pain as a natural and valid experience and take responsibility for it.

By holding yourself accountable, you can create the space and understanding necessary to delve deeper into the issue and uncover its root cause. This process of self-exploration allows you to work with your pain rather than fighting against it, leading to gradual healing and release from its grasp. With time, you may find that your pain becomes a source of wisdom and inspiration, helping you cultivate self-compassion, acceptance, and strength.

So, don't dismiss your pain or judge yourself for feeling it. Embrace it as an opportunity for self-discovery and growth, and let it guide you on your journey.

ARE YOU LIVING A LIFE *of Denial*?

Denial is a tempting refuge, an escape from facing the truth that awaits us. But is it truly living?

Yet, in denying our true selves, we rob life of its vibrant colors. We become sleepwalkers, traversing existence without truly seeing or experiencing its wonders. Disconnected from our emotions, we numb ourselves to the essence of our being, avoiding the aspects of life we dare not confront.

Grief has a way of leaving us feeling empty, disconnected from the world. Faced with such turbulent emotions, it is crucial to remain present. Opening ourselves to the surrounding reality allows us to reestablish our connection to ourselves and the world surrounding us.

If denial has become your shield for too long, it is time to confront the truth. Though it may be a painful pilgrimage, evading your emotions and sidestepping the obstacles that impede your growth will only perpetuate your suffering. To live a life of integrity and authenticity, we must be brave enough to acknowledge our wounds and fears.

Embrace the journey, for it may come with its share of challenges. Remember, transformation is not an overnight process; it requires time and intense dedication. But as you courageously confront your pain, you will uncover hidden wells of strength within. Say goodbye to denial and welcome the truth of your existence. With each intentional step, you carve a path toward a life filled with authenticity and purpose.

The path ahead may be arduous, but you are not alone. I am here to offer my unwavering support, accompanying you through every stride of this transformative journey. Embrace your inner resilience and have faith in the healing process.

Trust yourself and step boldly into a life of authenticity and growth. You have the power to rewrite your story.

The Guiding Light of *Embrace* Nurturing Those in Grief

Faced with another's grief, we often find ourselves at a loss for words. The profound pain and sorrow they bear can leave us powerless, uncertain of how to offer solace in their darkest hours. Yet, amidst the vastness of this challenge, there exists a flare of hope—a well-crafted grief book, EMBRACE.

In these pages, you'll find a companion journal that will bring comfort and understanding to those roaming the twisted path of sorrow.

While it is impossible to erase the pain, EMBRACE can soothe the aching heart and guide one's steps through the obstacles of grief.

The sentimental narratives make the emotions' kaleidoscope more explicit and the burden of grief more tolerable. As a treasured tool in your grief bag, the 7 Stages of Grief Alignment provides a roadmap for the griever and their companions, fostering awareness and healing.

Yet, it is crucial to remember that when supporting someone living in grief, the gift of your presence and enduring willingness to listen outweighs any words of wisdom or reassurance.

With its intricate nuances, grief often leaves those who mourn feeling isolated and misunderstood. EMBRACE is a heartfelt promise that assures you that you are not alone in your journey.

EMBRACE will offer hope and encouragement, reminding readers they are not alone in their sorrow. Consider giving them a copy to support a friend or loved one during grief.

If you want to support a friend or loved one during grief, consider giving them a copy of EMBRACE! You want the support of your loved ones, and the same goes for them needing you. As with any journey in life, the journey of grief as a team, we got this!

The Healing Dance of Grief
Nurturing the Spirit *within*

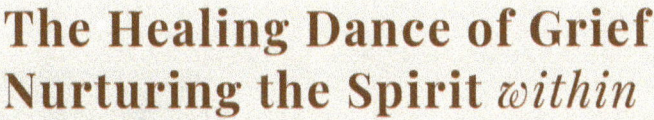

When someone close to us dies tragically, we are engulfed by an overwhelming sense of loss, accompanied by a symphony of painful emotions. We journey through this dimension of grief, uniquely navigating its twists and turns. Some shed tears like raindrops from a stormy sky, others ignite with fiery anger, while some retreat into the solitude of their inner world. These reactions, these expressions of grief, are the rivers that flow from the depths of our souls. We must honor them, for within these expressions lie the seeds of self-awareness and the catalysts for healing.

It's simple to feel disoriented and overwhelmed in today's fast-paced, ever-evolving society. The grieving process is a multifaceted test; we all long for the loving company of a compassionate that requires us to seek comfort from those who can relate. As a holistic practitioner, I stand ready with the tools and resources to accompany you on this sacred pilgrimage. Drawing upon my extensive experience, I offer a sanctuary where your voice can be heard, your story shared, and your healing ignited.

Discerning the way forward is exhausting in life's chaotic orchestra, where confusion and uncertainty reign. The weight of emotional pain may tempt us to forge ahead, mindlessly seeking an escape from the obstacles that hinder our progress. Yet, dear soul, a profound wellspring of resilience and strength lies within you. Developing spiritual growth can lead to a limitless abundance of peace and stability. Nurturing your connection with a higher power or the wisdom within you can help you navigate life's most brutal storms with grace and serenity. As you enter this sacred journey of spiritual expansion, you will uncover newfound capacities to navigate life's turbulent seas, supporting your passage and extending a loving hand to those who traverse similar paths.

The road may appear dimly lit as you tread its winding path. Yet, within you resides a radiance of faith, highlighting the darkness for those who desire comfort in your presence. Even when grief looms, keep hope alive in the sanctuary of your heart. I encourage optimism even in the darkness. Envision a shining star, your inner strength shining its light into the deepest crevices of despair. As you gaze upon the darkness, challenge fear and vulnerability to manifest and transform into a conduit for healing. By embracing the full spectrum of your being, shadows, and all, you control the destiny of self-empowerment. Even in the trenches of darkness, your intense light inspires and uplifts those who witness your strength and courage.

Remember that you are never alone in the sacred dance of grief, where each step is steeped with the essence of unconditional love. Reach out, Warrior, to those who can guide and support you on this transformative pilgrimage. Together, you will honor the pain, nurture your spirit, and spin a tapestry of healing that extends far beyond the realms of grief. Let the rhythm of your heart guide you, as it holds within it the tune of perseverance, the harmony of optimism, and the assurance of rejuvenation.

Shadows become tools that help shape Who You Are...

The Symphony of *Empathy* Navigating Responses to *Grief*

Why do some people run when I embrace my sadness?

Have you ever felt alone in your sadness because others choose to ignore or withdraw from you?

It's disheartening to question whether you deserve support or understanding. It can be challenging for those not accustomed to dealing with intense emotions like grief to face their feelings. Fear, unfamiliarity, and a lack of knowledge about responding supportively could all contribute to their feelings.

It can feel like others are trying to hide from the truth of your experience and being when they avoid hearing about your sorrowful tale. It might make you feel invisible, alone, and desperate for approval. An essential part of the grieving process is vulnerability, which searches for comfort in human connection and comprehension.

However, it is essential to note that only some can face and hold space for strong emotions, especially if they have not experienced something comparable. Their insecurity stems from a need for more ease with showing emotion. It's important not to take their reaction personally; instead, give yourself time and space to work through your feelings.

Be gentle with yourself and embrace the understanding that not everyone will comprehend or offer enduring support on this path. With time, you'll meet people who can hold the sacred space for your grief, opening doors to vital life lessons and opportunities for new relationships.

There can be many reasons why people don't respond to your melancholy expressions. Some people may struggle with displays of intense emotion, while others may feel ill-equipped to respond to someone who is deeply sorrowful. In certain instances, people may even fear that witnessing your sadness will awaken their dormant pain. It is essential to acknowledge that each person uniquely navigates grief, and adverse reactions to your sorrow do not show a lack of care or concern. Give them breathing room to deal with their feelings; they may discover the strength to help you.

As you continue your grief journey, remember that your emotions are valid and that your need for support is real. Seek solace in those who can hold space for your grief, and let go of the notion that everyone will understand. The dance of empathy requires patience and calls for self-compassion. If you care for yourself during this process, you show others how accepting melancholy can strengthen the spirit.

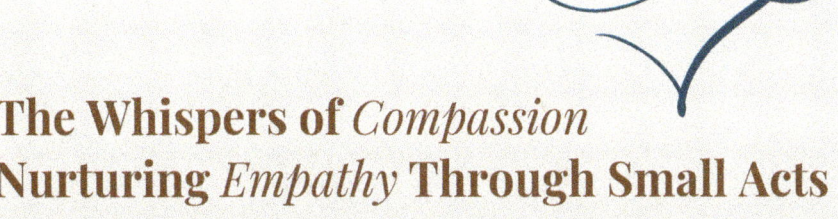

The Whispers of *Compassion*
Nurturing *Empathy* Through Small Acts

Empathy's complex webs of connection strengthen relationships during the grieving process. A kind touch, reassuring words, and a listening ear can go a long way toward alleviating emotional pain. During sadness, expressions of sympathy transform into a beautiful melody of support, kindness, and concern.

Even the tiniest gestures can convey the magnitude of affection and concern in moments of quiet reflection. Sincerity and love injected into the most straightforward actions can illuminate the darkest places. These seemingly insignificant acts go beyond words to bring solace to the soul. By doing these nice things for them, we can let them know they have our undying support and are not alone.

Sometimes, the answer lies not in words but in the silent embrace of companionship. To stand beside someone in their darkest hours to honor their wishes can transcend an act of compassion. You become a sanctuary of support for their wounded soul. Becoming a lifeline amidst the chaos by offering practical help, running errands, and preparing nourishing meals demonstrates that our warmth extends beyond mere words to sacred stillness.

They provide a sympathetic ear that accepts their suffering without judgment or making demands. We become instruments of compassion and wisdom, holding the door open for their recovery.

When words fail, being there and knowing how grateful we are can help comfort a broken spirit. Therefore, let us recognize the significance of greeting cards, reassuring embraces, and quiet moments of reflection. Aim to personify empathy, compassion, and concern. We become the vessels through which comfort is delivered, mending the broken parts of a mourning person's spirit in those quiet times.

> You can use the following phrases:
>
> My heart goes out to you; I'm sorry this is happening to you.
> "What is your loved one's name?"
> "What do you say we get some lunch together? Please tell me more about (insert name of cherished one here)."

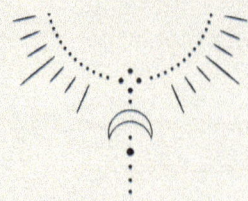

The Unseen Language of Sorrow
Embracing *Understanding* and *Letting Go*

It's frustrating when those close to you don't understand how much your loss means to you. Some wonder if avoiding those who can't share our sorrow is right. But let's PAUSE to think about this:

No matter how well you articulate your pain, not everyone can comprehend complex emotions. Despite our efforts to articulate our pain, some may struggle to grasp its true essence. In these situations, letting go of our dependence on their comprehension is not a sign of a lack of strength or inability. Our efforts to help them understand the inexplicable would be well-spent.

Don't you think it's wonderful to imagine a world where empathy is cultivated and understanding becomes a part of our collective etiquette? While that ideal may be far off, we can take comfort in the company of those who share our values and offer proper understanding and support. Seek comfort in knowing you are not alone on your grief journey. By doing so, we create space for our healing, allowing our sorrow to unfold in its way, guided by our resilience and the support of those who truly understand.

01
Let us find comfort in the arms of those who truly understand and share our pain on this developing path of sorrow. Even if others can't understand our pain, it's reassuring that some would listen with empathy and provide a safe place to heal.

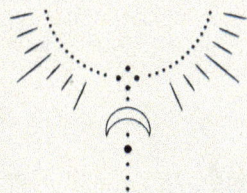

02

In the depths of sorrow, we are faced with a "griefosophical" lesson:

We are the chosen ones entrusted with the sacred duty of carrying the unseen language of sorrow. It is not a burden to bear but a calling that sets us apart from others. Our connection with our departed loved one runs deep, transcending the comprehension of others. The love we shared with them was unique, profound, and intimate, coloring our grief in hues that may mystify those who did not experience the same depth of connection.

Rather than harboring resentment or seeking understanding from those who cannot offer it, we can shift our perspective. It helps to think of ourselves as spiritual vessels that have solemnly promised to bear the burden of our grief. To mourn together is to witness the strength of love and reveal the depth of our connection.

By letting go of the expectation that everyone will understand our grief, we unlock a sense of communal understanding only discernible by our innermost beings. We become a collective source of higher consciousness. Our common grief language helps us bond with those who resonate with our vibe.

So, Warriors, Let up, hoping other people share your pain with you. Embrace the idea that you are connected to a group of people who "get it," and you become a force that cannot be stopped together. Make use of your suffering as a starting point for introspection and growth.

In doing so, you give tribute to the unconditional love you shared with your departed loved one and become that twinkle who walks this path of grief.

> In grief, we are chosen to carry the unseen language of sorrow, a testament to our love and resilience.

Unveiling the Art of Respecting *Grief*

In this era of digital connectivity, we find ourselves conditioned to swiftly move on and brush aside the depths of our grief. Glossing over the importance of grieving and grief acceptance might be easy in today's fast-paced world. However, grief encompasses far more than prolonged sadness; it is an emotional journey that demands time, reverence, empathy, and patience to mend.

Loss, especially the irreparable loss of love, is at the heart of mourning. When we suffer a profound loss, it changes who we are and shines a light on what gives our lives true purpose. The path to recovery and growth lies in sincerely accepting our suffering.

Nobody enjoys being hurt, and most people will try to avoid it. However, suffering is a part of being human and must be faced head-on. Grief and loss, and the emotional sorrow they cause, are experiences all humans share at some point. Neither can we expect anybody else to take away our suffering, but we can show compassion, which can teach us a great deal about how to deal with the misery of others. Through compassion, we see that the suffering of others is natural and merits our whole attention.

The ability to empathize with others serves as a helpful reminder that there is no single "correct" way to deal with suffering. It is unnecessary to have all the solutions to be compassionate; all we need to do is be there for people when they are suffering.

So, when we see a loved one going through a tough time, let's not rush to ease their suffering. Instead, let's give our undivided attention to becoming wise. By doing so, we show them the kindness and consideration they deserve. There is an act of tremendous bravery, tenacity, and grit at the heart of mourning, an act that teaches profound truths about what it is to be human. So, let's not rush past the remembrances of limitless, unconditional LOVE.

Embracing the *Everlasting* Journey

BOTTOM *line*

One of life's greatest challenges is coming to terms with the fact that mourning is never really "done." We may reach a point where the raw pain of our loss has begun to fade, but the scars remain. These scars can be a source of strength and comfort. They remind us of the loved ones we have lost and help us appreciate life's fragility.

But keep in mind that you will never fully "get over" your loss. It is an ongoing journey that we all must travel. There may be days when the path is smooth and the going is rough. But eventually, we will reach our destination: a place where we can find peace and happiness again.

Healing is an ever-unfolding journey, an intricate dance of self-discovery and growth. As we set out on our journey, we recognize that our wounds are not who we are but a testament to our capacity to love fiercely and persevere through adversity. Unconditional self-love feeds the soul and opens the door to healing on all levels. Putting aside baggage and focusing on what brings us joy might help us find inner freedom.

You may find that your relationship with your loved one changes as you move through grief. Their presence becomes a source of strength and comfort, reminding you of their eternal love. You gradually rebuild your life as you heal, carrying their memory within you. Their spirit entwines with yours, illuminating the path to a meaningful existence.

While healing may never be complete, grief can propel you toward a more positive emotional journey. Embracing and expressing your grief healthily allows for soul healing to begin.

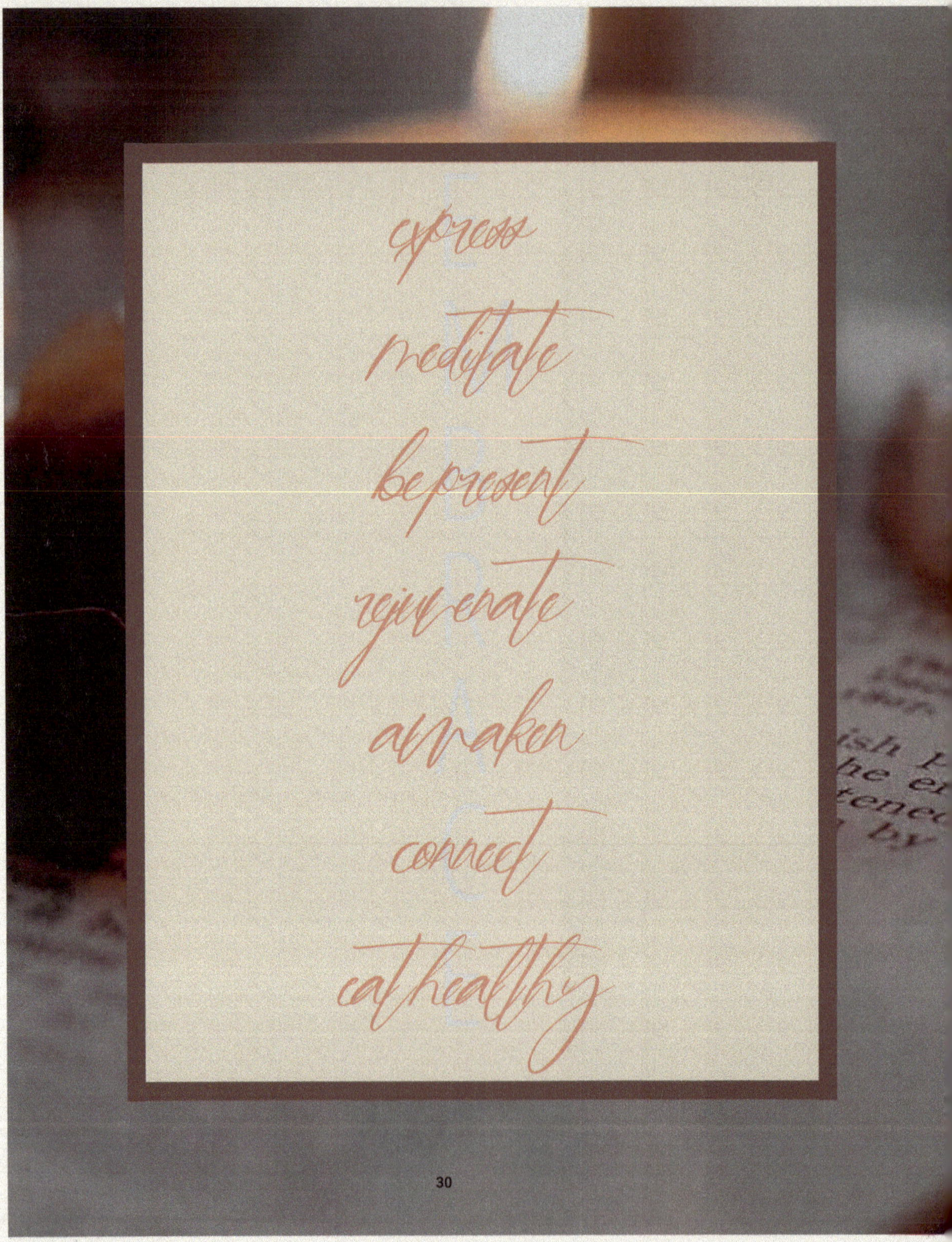

express

meditate

be present

rejuvenate

awaken

connect

eat healthy

DOES EMBRACE
Speak to You?

Explore the transformative power of The 7 Stages of GRIEF Alignment workbook journal, designed to support you authentically and effectively on your grief journey. Each stage of this journal is carefully crafted to nurture your physical and mental well-being, empowering you to strengthen critical aspects of your health as you navigate through the aftermath of a traumatic event. Embracing these stages will lead you to greater strength, resilience, and a revitalized sense of purpose.

Drawing from personal experiences of loss and trauma, I created the 7 Stages of GRIEF Alignment mini journal to assist those willing to EMBRACE in their healing process. Within its pages, you'll discover practices that have deeply impacted my grief journey, enabling me to navigate through the pain and embrace genuine growth mindfully. These practices have brought about timeless healing, from releasing old attachments to rebuilding a lost sense of unconditional love.

This eternal healing perfectly captures the beauty of "Healing."

Whether at the beginning of your grief journey or making progress, embracing the stages outlined in this journal can ease the burden and infuse joy into your life. Let's say you've had enough and are ready to start living again. Please join me on the 7 Stages of the GRIEF Alignment workbook journal's transformational journey, or go even further and earn your Certified Wellness Warrior designation.

Take a deep breath, stay resilient, and remember that even in the darkest moments, we possess the inner strength to move forward. Embrace this opportunity and witness its profound impact on your life. Not doing so would be a mistake.

EXPRESS

Welcome to the First Stage of Grief Alignment: Express. In this stage, we encourage you to unleash your thoughts, feelings, and trauma through emotional journaling. By embracing this practice, you voice your emotions and release anxiety, triggers, and pain.

Reflect on its meaning in your grief journey and explore its significance. Use your notebook as a place of refuge where you may explore who you are and how you got here. Allow your own words to heal and shape your spirit.

Three ways you can integrate 'Express' into your daily therapy:

Emotional Journaling	**Artistic Expression**	**Verbal Communication**
Write freely each day to express and process your emotions.	Engage in creative activities to communicate and release emotions.	Share your feelings with a trusted person or practitioner for support and validation.

Expression is the key to unlocking our connection, allowing us to co-create a reality rooted in love and acceptance. So say their name, share your story, feel every moment, and remember—you are here for a reason. And always remember—you are here with a purpose. You have the power to create. So keep expressing yourself—you have everything it takes to thrive!

How will you express today?

MEDITATE

Have you ever explored the richness of meditation? It offers a gateway to discovering tranquility and clarity in grief or challenging moments. By dedicating time to cultivating mindful awareness, we unlock the potential for remarkable revelations.
With each intentional inhalation and exhalation, we create a sacred space within ourselves, allowing us to confront our emotions from a higher perspective.

Discover peace in nature's embrace, where meditation unveils transformative insights.

Pause for a moment and ask yourself: When was the last time you truly paused and immersed yourself in the vivid reality of "here"? It is in the here and now, the ever-present moment, where true existence lives. It is within this moment that the miracle of life unfolds.

BE PRESENT

'Be Present' is the 3rd Stage of Grief Alignment, encouraging us to be still. Society often expects us to conform to specific standards, but we have the power to within ourselves begin a path toward wellness simply by showing up.

Being present allows us to reconnect with life, love, and feel again.

Let's focus on being present and mindful. Pay attention to your breath - feel the rise and fall of your chest and let it move like a symphony's crescendo. Focus on the present and feel the caress of each inhale and exhale. Take in the vibrant feelings that sweep your entire being, and let them merge with the present moment.

Allowing your emotions to take over can be liberating. Accepting and working with our feelings without hesitation or judgment is crucial. Whatever those emotions may be, it's okay to feel them. Take a moment to permit yourself to step back, allowing your soul to have time within this very breath.

REJUVENATE

For true revitalization, we must turn inward and examine our bodily, mental, and spiritual states.

It can help us reclaim our vitality and lead us toward joy and fulfillment, especially when dealing with the loss of a loved one or the constant stresses of modern life. Transformation comes with self-reflection, inner growth, and healing. You have the power to do this!

By embracing new challenges and striving to grow in every aspect of our lives, we can reignite the spark and fire up our souls. So, why wait? We can rejuvenate and awaken joy at every level with determination and self-acceptance.

Reflecting on our loved ones and the gifts they gave us can also help rejuvenate our lives in their honor. Whether remembering a favorite memory or reaching out to those who supported us during difficult times, each act deepens the connection between us and our loved ones, even as they move beyond the physical world.

Ultimately, we choose how to react to grief, but by acknowledging our journey and embracing joy, we can find strength in our spirit again.

AWAKEN

In the 5th Stage of Grief Alignment, Awaken, you are invited to embrace the essence of being fully alive and anchored in the present moment. Retaining and shielding ourselves from raw emotions and harsh realities is expected in the depths of grief.

Awakening is the key that unlocks the door to our inner resilience and rekindles our faith in the truth that lies before us.

Pause and contemplate your life as it stands today. Allow this fresh perspective to offer a broader view, enabling you to observe your journey from a distance. In this introspection, you may realize that all you need lives within, and a vast expanse of possibilities awaits you on the horizon.

Let's embrace the awakening, as it acts as a catalyst that propels us forward with a renewed sense of vitality and purpose on our journey.

CONNECT

In the 'C' of EMBRACE, we find the power of connection in the 6th Stage of Grief. As we make our way through the complexities of this world, now is the moment to strengthen our connection to ourselves, our spirit, and our mind. While it may pose challenges, remember that we all thrive on daily connections.

How will you choose to CONNECT today?

Your mind. Your body. Your spirit.

Make a conscious effort to connect with yourself by dedicating just five minutes to express gratitude, a walk in nature, engaging in reflective journaling, cooking, creating, or allowing yourself to be still. Focus on self-care and self-reflection to enhance your well-being.

Tune in to your needs and honor them, for it is in these connections that true healing and growth can flourish.

EAT HEALTHY

In the final stage of our grief alignment journey, we are called to embrace the importance of nourishing ourselves through healthy eating. As we have journeyed through the different stages of grief in our course, we have learned the significance of addressing our emotional, mental, and spiritual needs. Now, we focus on the physical aspect of our well-being, recognizing that what we put into our bodies directly impacts our healing process.

Eating healthy becomes the inner thread that weaves all the stages of our grief alignment journey. By nourishing ourselves with wholesome, nutrient-rich foods, we provide our bodies with the fuel to support our healing from the inside out. We actively participate in our healing process by prioritizing foods promoting strength, vitality, and well-being.

As we continue our journey beyond grief, let us carry healthy eating lessons. Let us embrace the power of wholesome foods to support our ongoing healing and growth.

It is through this holistic approach that we can truly thrive and create a life that is vibrant, nourished, and filled with joy.

YOUR INNER
spiritual warrior!

EMBRACE is the ultimate exhilarating journey of healing and transformation. This course is not just a certification—it is a profound commitment to healing and a powerful dedication to moving forward with purpose.

We encounter countless challenges that test our resilience and tempt us to give up. Yet, deep within us lies an untapped well of strength, waiting patiently to be discovered and unleashed. This course empowers you to tap into that inner strength, unlock your full potential, and become the vessel to *healing it forward*.

The key lies in listening to your heart and trusting your instincts. By tuning into the untapped wisdom at the core of your being, you gain the clarity and guidance needed to navigate any obstacle that comes your way. With a resilient focus, you cultivate the courage and determination required to **move with** emotional barriers.

As you EMBRACE this journey, you discover that nurturing your inner world positively impacts your external world, cultivating meaningful connections with others, and investing in your self-enlightenment. The key lies in listening to your heart and trusting your instincts.

The 7 Stages of Grief Alignment will be your guiding light as you EMBRACE each stage of grief in your own time. Recognize that these stages are not linear processes; you may move back and forth between them as you navigate your unique grief journey. This flexibility allows you to honor your experience and progress at your own pace.

Are you ready to step into your power as a Certified Grief Wellness Coach?
Sign up today and trust your inner calling, take that leap of faith, and let your guiding light illuminate the path of healing and transformation for yourself and others.

A Graceful Pivot to Purpose

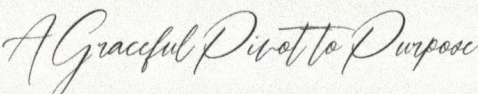

EXPRESS
The First Stage of Grief

EMBRACE

MICHELE C. BELL
THE GRIEF WARRIOR®

you've made it

You are now ready to **EMBRACE** our First Stage:

— *express* —

That's the blessing and power of **pivoting with purpose.**

What are the 7 Stages of Grief Alignment?
Express. **M**editate.
Be Present. **R**ejuvenate.
Awaken. **C**onnect. **E**at Healthy.

Healing begins with acceptance, and alignment transforms us through embracing our circumstances.

The empower of embracing is in your next chapter –
are you ready to turn the page?

Table of Contents

Express Our First Step	03
Lesson 1. - How Writing Can Help Heal Loss	05
Lesson 2. - Dealing With Change	10
Lesson 3 - Remembering Moments Before Loss	14
Lesson 4 - Dealing With Painful Memories	18
Lesson 5 - Express What Your Loss Means to You	22
Lesson 6 - Eliminated Grief	27
Lesson 7 - Taking Notice of Coincidences	31
Lesson 8 - A Message From Your Loved One	37
Lesson 9 - The Burning Letter: Ritual for Release	41
Lesson 10 - The Power of Connection & Healing	45

EXPRESS
our first step

Navigating through loss and grief is undeniably one of the most arduous journeys in a person's life. It is common to retreat and bury these emotions deep within instinctively. Yet, the weight of this burden doesn't dissipate with time unless addressed genuinely and compassionately. We genuinely require abundant love, expression, and mindful attention for healing.

Harnessing the Power of Writing for Healing During Grief

Accepting and acknowledging the emotions of grief is a vital step toward healing. You unlock the potential for profound transformation by actively listening to your feelings. Writing is a powerful tool in this journey, enabling a deeper understanding and appreciation of your emotions and fostering growth amidst the pain.

In this course, you will engage in transformative writing practices, authentically expressing your heartfelt feelings. Through this process, you will better understand your emotions, giving them the space they deserve. Embracing this healing practice, you embark on a journey of self-discovery, navigating the depths of grief and finding solace through understanding.

This course includes:

- Nine lessons – each including writing exercises and questions to self-reflect on
- Expert grief guidance and lessons on how to use writing to channel your feelings
- Guidance on how to write from the heart
- Tried and tested methods to move past the grief and heal
- Self-reflection on loss and where it has taken you

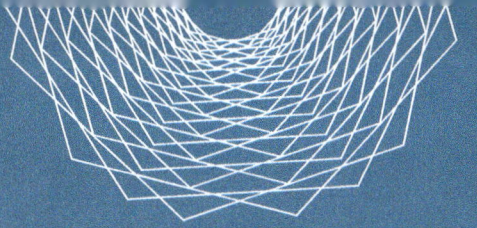

You should take this course if:

- You have painful and repressed memories
- You recently experienced a loss or grief
- You wish to understand your feelings better
- You want to learn how to use writing to FEEL
- You want to address the loss of a loved one
- You want to find peace

This interactive journal workbook is designed to help you express your feelings, providing a safe and nurturing space to articulate your pain, reflect on your experiences, and chart your progress toward healing. By using writing as an outlet, you'll be able to draw from your inner strength, transforming your energy into a powerful tool for healing.

"I am Living Proof a Broken Heart Can Still Live"

The Grief Warrior

Write a mantra you can return to when you feel overwhelmed by grief.
_____
_____
_____
_____

"Say Their Name" in a quote.
_____
_____
_____
_____

LESSON 1 How Writing Can Help *to* Heal Loss

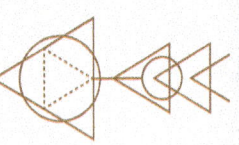

Experiencing loss can profoundly affect every aspect of your life. The absence of a loved one can leave a void that seems impossible to fill. The mind grapples to understand the enormity of the loss; your heart yearns for the one who is no longer there; stress permeates your body; and your spirit may feel as though it's in a state of turmoil. Navigating this emotional landscape can be overwhelming.

Healing from such profound grief is a journey that takes time. There often comes a moment—a turning point—when the weight of the loss becomes too heavy to bear. At this juncture, the void begins to fill with love and peace. To reach this point of transformation, self-expression becomes a vital tool.

Understanding and articulating your feelings is the first step toward healing. Expressing these emotions through words can be incredibly therapeutic, transforming your pain into a catalyst for growth. Many find solace in writing, as it provides a private, peaceful, and intimate space for authentic self-expression that originates from the soul.

Writing is a holistic process that integrates your body, mind, spirit, and emotions, uniting them in a common goal: healing. It allows you to channel your pain, replacing it with positive energy as you journey toward overcoming your loss.

Writing is more than just moving your hand across a page. It's a deep dive into your emotions, memories, and sensory experiences. It's about transforming your life experiences into words, giving a tangible form to your grief and a pathway to healing. Embrace the power of writing and embark on your journey toward healing and peace.

> At every point in the human journey, We find that we have to let go in order to move forward; And letting go means dying a little. In the process, We are being created anew, Awakened afresh to the Source of our being.
>
> — *Natalie Goldberg*

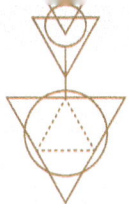

Once upon a time, in the heart of a storm called Loss, a mind was lost in a labyrinth of confusion, desperately seeking understanding and answers. As the storm began to subside, the mind transformed into a sanctuary, where answers slowly unfolded like the petals of a blooming flower.

Amid the storm, a heart reached out, yearning for the one taken too soon. As the skies cleared, the heart, like a skilled architect, began to rebuild itself piece by piece, each brick a testament to resilience and love.

Initially seeking shelter from the storm of stress, the body began to find its strength as healing took root. It transformed into a powerhouse, fueling the journey toward the dawn of healing. The spirit, initially lost in the storm's vastness, gradually found its way to become a lighthouse, radiating inspiration as the healing sun began to rise.

In this tale, *Pain*, the most disorienting and bewildering character, cannot be overcome by the body or mind alone. It required a collective effort to pool all inner resources and pull together towards a shared goal—the healing sunrise.

On this journey, writing emerged as a powerful ally. It empowered the characters to articulate their feelings, converse with the loved one they've lost, and dialogue with their past, present, and future selves. It allowed them to take control of their narrative and shape their memories and experiences into a story of resilience and growth.

What lessons can you embrace from this story?

Where did this story fit into the tapestry of their lives? Reflecting on these questions, let your thoughts flow.

if you haven't tried, you haven't lived

Letters of Love

All the writing for this course should be written in your Warrior Journal, a sacred space for your thoughts, emotions, and reflections. Your Warrior Journal is a sanctuary where your words can flow freely. It's a space to express your deepest feelings, knowing they will be held confidently. You can revisit your writings whenever you wish, to add to them, alter them, or even erase them. This is your journey, and your journal reflects your path.

Choose a serene and comfortable space for your writing sessions, away from the world's distractions. Let this be a place where you can focus on your thoughts and emotions, away from the interruptions of everyday life. Remember, there's no rush on this journey.

A Letter to Your Beloved:
A Heartfelt Beginning to Your Healing Journey

Take a deep breath, find a quiet space, and let your heart guide your pen. It's time to write a letter to your loved one. Begin with a simple, heartfelt salutation:

"Dear, My Love, My _____," and fill in the blank with the name of your loved one.

This is your moment to reconnect, reminisce, and express everything in your heart. Share your cherished memories, the moments that made you laugh, the times that brought you closer. Tell them what they meant to you, what they still mean to you. Let your words paint a picture of your shared journey, of the love that continues to live in your heart.

Don't worry about the perfect words, the perfect grammar, or the perfect punctuation. This is not about perfection; it's about expression. It's about raw, honest, heartfelt communication. Let your words flow freely; let them come straight from your heart.

"Let your heart guide your pen on this journey of healing. In every letter, every word, every memory shared, you're not just expressing your grief; you're honoring your love."

Michele Bell

AS WE DRAW TODAY'S LESSON TO A CLOSE, I INVITE YOU TO REFLECT ON THESE THREE CONSIDERATIONS:

Reflection: How did the process of writing the letter make you feel? Did it bring up any new emotions or insights about your grief?

_____
_____
_____
_____

Expression: Were any thoughts or feelings you found particularly challenging to express in your letter? How might you approach these in your future writing?

_____
_____
_____
_____

Connection: Did you feel connected with your loved one in writing the letter? How can you continue to nurture this connection in your healing journey?

_____
_____
_____
_____

"In every heartfelt letter, we find a bridge to our loved ones, a pathway to healing, and a testament to the enduring power of love."

Michele Bell

I encourage you to pen as many letters as your heart desires. As we conclude today's lesson, I invite you to take at least 60 seconds to CONNECT with the process. Remember, you're not just going through this process but actively shaping it. You are strong. You are powerful. You are in control. And above all, you are empowered.

LESSON 2   Dealing *with* Change

Every soul dances to the rhythm of loss in its unique way. For some, the dance begins abruptly, the music of loss striking a sudden, discordant note. The melody unfolds slowly for others, a haunting tune that lingers over time. Some of us, with an intuitive ear, can hear the faint strains of the song even before it fully begins.

Take a moment to remember when the music first reached you.

This moment, this first note of your loss, is the starting point of your journey. It's the foundation upon which you'll write your letters this week. It's the moment when the landscape of your life shifts, and the world takes on a different hue. Things will never be the same, and acknowledging this change is crucial to your healing process.

Take a moment to jot down any thoughts from this reflection.

Your memories are the melodies that will guide you on this journey. They are the notes that compose the song of your healing. Embrace them with resonance; they are the notes guiding you toward healing.

So, let the music play, let your pen dance on the paper, and let your healing journey begin.

Navigating the Uncharted: Making Sense of Loss

Humans are wired to seek understanding and find patterns and logic in the world around us. Though small, our minds are vast in their capacity to problem-solve and guide us through life's challenges. We lean on our intellect in times of need, trusting it to illuminate our path.

Yet, it's important to remember that it's okay to feel lost and not to have all the answers. Grief is not a problem to be solved but a journey to be traveled. And as you journey through your loss, know that you are seen, you are heard, and you are not alone.

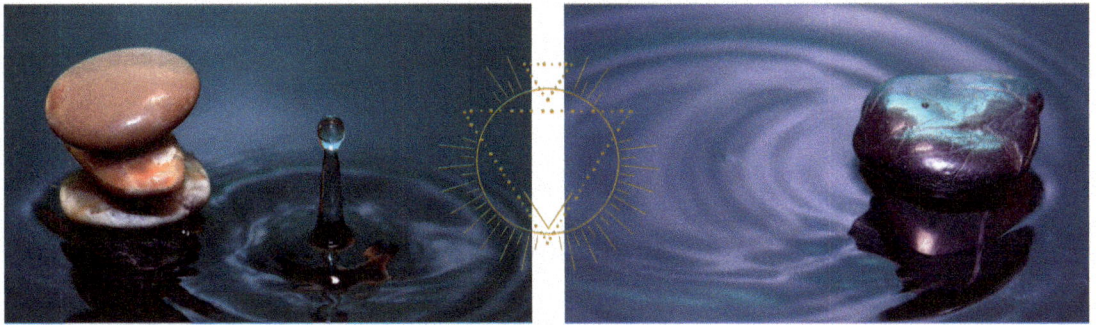

In the wake of grief, loss, and trauma, even your body may seem to retreat, conserving energy as it navigates the unfamiliar landscape of sorrow. You've witnessed a chapter of your life transition from the present to the past, a shift that can be challenging to comprehend. Many of us turn to a higher power, seeking solace in religious or spiritual beliefs during these times.

In its gentle rhythm, writing can serve as a beacon of light in these moments of darkness. It can help you:

- Understand Your Loss
- Find peace in your belief system
- Uncover the 'Why'
- Pause, Observe, Reflect, Heal

Your Spiritual Journey:

When you experience a sudden and extreme change, you must find a way to rebuild. However, writing can be a gateway to finding perspective. You can never find peace until you understand your loss.

For those with religious or spiritual beliefs, these can provide solace in times of need. Loss often unearths feelings we were unaware of, such as hidden regrets. On the other hand, you may find yourself without guilt, a fortunate position that brings its form of peace.

How do we cope when a loved one is no longer with us? The beauty of our human experience is that we can connect with those no longer physically present. Through our imagination and visions, we can engage in conversations, revisit shared experiences, and keep our memories alive. This doesn't signify madness but our deep human need for connection.

Writing to or about your loved one can provide immense comfort. It allows you to revisit cherished memories, find closure, and maintain a connection. Throughout this course, you'll be encouraged to use your imagination for healing and write letters that bridge the gap between loss and love.

Writing to your lost one or about them can be exceptionally comforting, giving you a sense of closure and looking back on fond memories. Remember, the path ahead is new, but you're not alone. Your feelings are seen, your experiences are valid, and your story matters.

Letters of Love

Take a deep breath, find a quiet space, and let your heart guide your pen. It's time to write a letter to your loved one. Begin with a simple, heartfelt salutation:
*Please find a photograph of your loved one and place it before you.

Dear _____, One feeling I've felt coming up a lot lately is...

_____
_____
_____
_____
_____
_____
_____
_____

As We Conclude Today's Journey, Reflect on These Three Considerations:

If I could forgive my loved one for something, it would be...

_____
_____
_____
_____

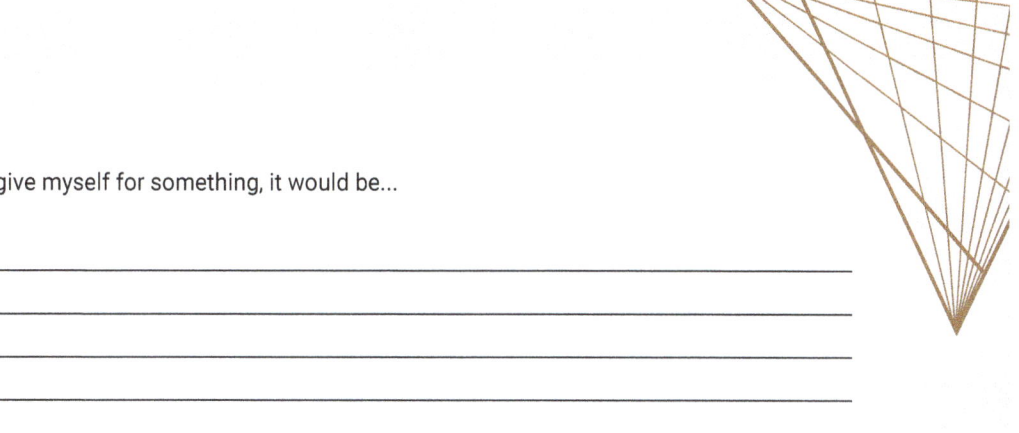

If I could forgive myself for something, it would be...

___

How can you turn these raw emotions into a positive experience?

___

30 Days of Connection: A Healing Journey

For the next 30 days, write a letter to your loved one each morning and evening. Share your daily experiences, thoughts, and memories. On a full moon night, find a peaceful spot outdoors or create a serene space indoors with a white candle and an earthing mat. Read one of your letters aloud, imagining your loved one beside you, sharing this moment. Through this practice, you will feel seen, heard, and connected on your path to healing.

LESSON 3

Remembering Moments *before* Loss

When we experience a loss, our initial state is usually shocking. Our minds struggle to comprehend the absence of someone or something significant, and we feel numb emotionally and physically. Expressing the loss in words can be difficult during the first few hours and days.

As we attempt to return to our daily routine, reminders of the loss can flood our minds unexpectedly and bring us back to despair. These memories contain messages that are crucial to our healing process. Ignoring them could lead us to get stuck in a cycle of grief. However, sharing these memories can give us the power to overcome our pain.

"Everybody needs his memories. They keep the wolf of insignificance from the door."

— K. R. Fischer

Unearthing Memories: A Journey Through Time

As you allow memories to surface, you may experience some for the first time. However, most people dealing with loss will be able to name their repeated memories off the top of their heads. These memories often pop up regularly and can bring both pain and happiness. Pleasant and painful memories are equally important and worthy of being written about.

Take time, find a comfortable sitting spot, and reflect on your memories before experiencing a significant loss. What initially comes to mind? It's helpful to take note of these memories as they surface organically, without any pressure to force them.

In today's lesson, there won't be any letter-writing assignments. Instead, the task is to organize these memories in a natural order—in a way that feels natural to you. After you create a list of positive and negative recollections, please keep it in a safe place for future lessons. You are adding more nuggets to your journey!

Art Therapy Homework
7 day challenge

Here are the supplies you will need:

- Colored tissue paper, which you can use to represent the various emotions you are feeling now.
- A journal, scrapbook, or some paper.
- Colored markers.
- Glue, paintbrush, and glaze.

one

Create a list of emotions you are feeling. Some common grief emotions are despair, anxiety, guilt, anger, denial, fear, isolation, loneliness, sadness, numbness, etc. Positive emotions can be like joy, gratitude, love, and hope.

_____

_____

two
Tear off each colored tissue relating to the emotion you are feeling daily.

three
Write down the emotion next to the colored tissue paper.

four
Complete the entire page to represent the colors of emotions you are experiencing.

five
Be creative each day. Place into a collage. That's it! Glue and Glaze.

art therapy homework

This assignment helps create each day's page to represent the current combination of emotions you are experiencing. Morning or evening is recommended to commit yourself to this assignment.

It helps visually show the ebbs and flows of different emotions over time.

You can also create this design on an empty wall in your home!

Let your pen flow across your journal, each word a step towards healing.

What does moving toward your pain mean to you?

In our healing journey, we often encounter the concept of moving toward our pain. But what does this truly mean to you? This isn't about dwelling in sorrow but acknowledging it, understanding it, and learning from it.

Take a moment to reflect on this idea. **How do you perceive this movement toward your pain? What emotions or thoughts does it evoke?**

Consider a moment when you consciously chose to move toward your pain. **What did you learn from this experience? How did it contribute to your healing process?**

Remember, your perspective is unique and valuable. Through this reflection, you are seen and heard, and your experiences are acknowledged.

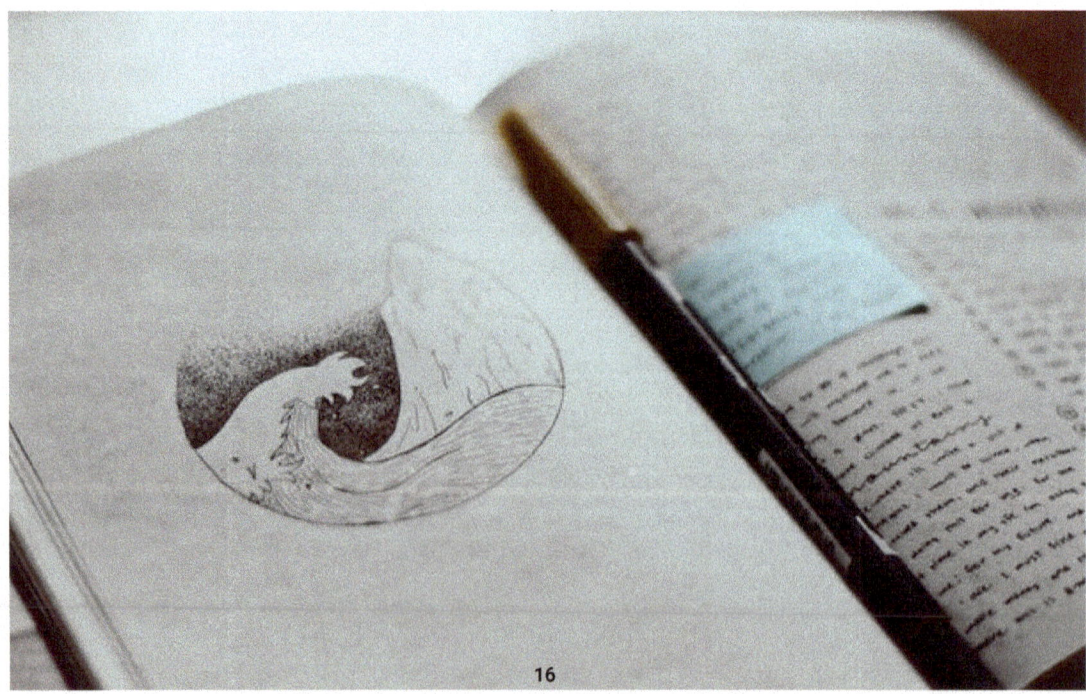

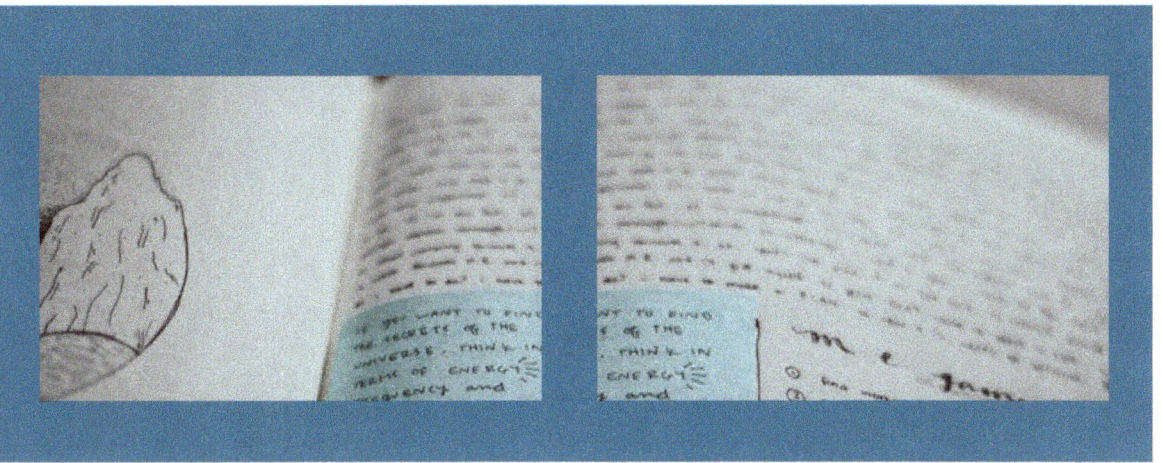

As you end each day's lesson, take a moment to reflect, an invitation to healing. Your grief, with its unique rhythm of pain, will continue to seek your attention, gently urging you to embrace it, bit by bit.

How is the pain of your grief seeking your attention?
In its profound depth, grief often communicates with us subtly. It nudges us, seeking our attention.
So, how is the pain of your grief reaching out to you?
Take a moment to reflect on this. **Are there specific moments, thoughts, or feelings that amplify your grief? Are there certain triggers that bring your pain to the forefront?**

Remember, your grief is a part of your journey, not an obstacle to be overcome. You are taking a crucial step toward healing by acknowledging and understanding its signals.

List the changes you've noticed due to your current challenges.

These could be related to our sense of self, such as confidence, identity, health, or personality changes. They could impact our sense of security, affecting our emotional stability, financial situation, or lifestyle. They could even touch upon our understanding of meaning, altering our faith, dreams, goals, or joy.

Once you've identified these losses, choose one or two that resonate deeply with you. Write about each one, exploring their impact on your life and your feelings towards these changes.

Imagine you could ask these changes one question. What would it be?

Ask EACH change, "How can I learn to adapt to you?" or "What lessons are you here to teach me?" or even "How can I find peace between the twists and turns of these changes?"

LESSON 4

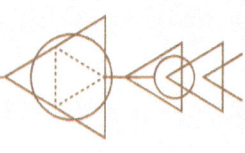

Dealing *with* Painful Memories

We've explored memories over the past three lessons, including some that may have caused us pain. We have also found that acknowledging and accepting these emotions can help lessen the pain. Writing to your loved ones and discussing these feelings and memories can bring comfort.

When we experience loss, some of us may want to forget, but another part of us may resist doing so. It's important to recognize that we can't truly move forward without releasing the pain, but that doesn't mean it's easy. Letting go of the pain can feel like letting go of the person, which can be confusing and overwhelming.

This can be an extremely confusing time. As we *move with*, please acknowledge any reluctance to let go of your writing if you feel the urge to. This is a reminder to be mindful of these feelings, as accepting them is an integral part of the creative and healing process. Take your time and allow yourself to find positivity in the healing process, which will ultimately help you move forward.

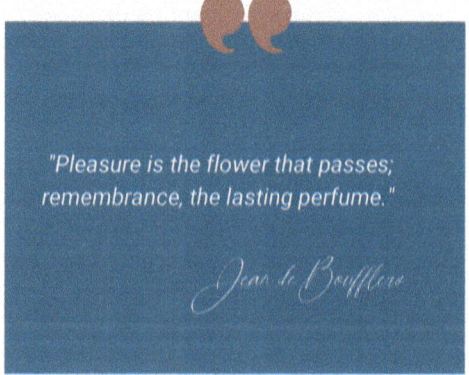

"Pleasure is the flower that passes; remembrance, the lasting perfume."

Jean de Boufflers

The Metamorphosis of Memories: From Sorrow to Serenity

Memories, even the most painful ones, can be rewritten. They can transform to evolve into something meaningful, even positive, over time.

Consider, for instance, the sudden loss of a family member in a car accident. The tragedy was so overwhelming that every car, every road became a stark reminder of the loss. Our shared love for automobiles, once a source of joy and connection, seemed to be overshadowed by the enormity of the grief.

Yet, as time passed and the raw edges of the loss began to soften, a shift occurred. You could revisit the cherished memories we had created together, tinkering with our grandfather's car in his old, dusty garage. The laughter, the camaraderie - these memories began to resurface, their light piercing through the veil of grief.

While still present, the loss sting wasn't as severe. The space created made room for positive memories, allowing them to coexist. This journey is a valuable lesson about the resilience of the human spirit and the importance of cherishing life's fleeting moments while we can.

In writing the therapeutic potential of writing is a well-documented phenomenon. Many renowned authors have attested to the role of writing in navigating their mental health journeys. Writing serves as a compass, guiding them through the complex maze of their emotions.
.
When confronted with a traumatic loss, our brain often captures a visual snapshot of the moment, a poignant still frame that the smallest things can trigger.

Yet, when we translate our experiences into words, we create a space to confront and understand our loss. Writing allows us to dissect our pain, view it from different angles, and, ultimately, lessen its impact.

If left unaddressed, the pain can continue to grow, casting a long shadow over our lives. But when we engage the written side of our brain, we initiate a healing process.

Words become our allies, helping us navigate the terrain of trauma and loss. Many have walked this path before us, and their experiences show us the incredible transformational power of writing.

Writing Memories

To minimize distractions, you may consider moving to a comfortable and safe space, like your sacred sanctuary. When you are ready to reminisce about your loved one, begin writing:

Dear _____, no matter how hard I try, I cannot forget this memory, and I wanted to talk to you today...

_____
_____
_____
_____
_____
_____
_____
_____
_____

PLEASE USE A JOURNAL TO WRITE DOWN AN INTUITIVE PROMPT

**As you conclude, pause and reflect on these three thoughts:
Reflect on the emotional landscape painted by their presence in your life.**

I feel the strongest sense of connection with my loved one when....

_____
_____
_____
_____
_____
_____
_____
_____

Journey back to a moment shared with your loved one that sparked laughter. Can you recall the details of that moment? Where were you both? What words were spoken? What actions led to the outburst of joy?

_____
_____
_____
_____
_____
_____
_____
_____
_____

How did the presence of your loved one stir emotions within you? Were there specific instances where their actions or words kindled a particular feeling?

_____
_____
_____
_____
_____
_____
_____
_____
_____

If you have more than one memory to share today, feel free to write multiple letters in your journal. You can use the prompts given above to write another letter.

Writing is healing

LESSON 5

Express What Your Loss Means *to* You

Navigating through the aftermath of a loss can feel like walking through a fog, where everything familiar suddenly becomes unclear. It's a harsh reminder of how quickly life can change and how joy can unexpectedly turn into sorrow. The absence left by losing someone or something important can create a deep sense of emptiness. But we begin to see the first signs of healing in recognizing this loss and facing this emptiness.

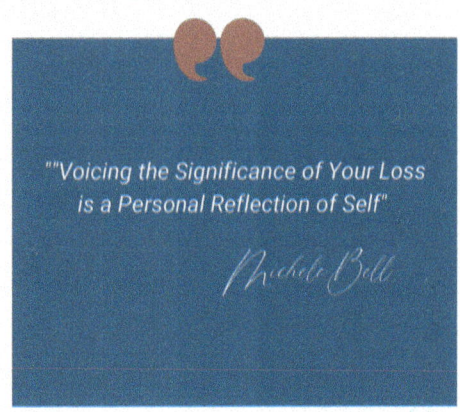

""Voicing the Significance of Your Loss is a Personal Reflection of Self"

Michele Bell

Take a moment to reflect on the depth of your loss. Beyond the irreplaceable individual, what else has been taken away? Are there emotional echoes that continue to resonate within you? Has it altered the rhythm of your daily life, reshaped your conversations, or changed your plans? As you journey through the grieving process, allow yourself to explore these aspects, for they, too, form part of your story of loss.

Life flashes by in an instant, so it is essential to take the time to enjoy the little things, like smelling the first flowers of spring. It can often feel like juggling many balls simultaneously while pausing to enjoy something else is seemingly impossible.

However, it is time for this lesson to put the balls down momentarily. This is about savoring those sweet smells.

Capturing precisely what you have lost in words is nearly impossible. There are so many things, memories, and emotions that cannot be described. It isn't just about who a person was to you; it is about how they enriched your life and the void they have left behind.

Of course, living with their essence every day was an effortless pleasure, but living without them is hard. Now it is time to let your loved one know it's not about how they died; it's about how they lived that brought JOY into your existence.

Use the following as a library of ideas to spark your memory.

The loss of a person/animal:

- The harmony you had
- How they improved your life
- How they helped
- How they hindered
- What you shared
- What conflicts you had
- What resolutions you found
- What you remember most
- First impression
- Final memory
- How did they make you proud?
- How did you make them proud?
- Something you never knew
- Something you wish you could ask
- The one thing you would do with them now

The loss of health:

- What you took for granted
- How you have changed since
- A gift from the loss
- Why it is hard to live without
- What you have learned from it
- What you would change
- What you can no longer do
- Advice for others

The loss of a job:

- What you lost
- Why you loved it
- Why you hated it
- What it gave you
- What you miss most
- What you have learned since
- What do you want next?

USE YOUR JOURNAL TO WRITE DOWN INTUITIVE PROMPTS

Jot down any memories triggered by these prompts and save them for future reference. These notes will be valuable when you write letters to departed loved ones, particularly when expressing gratitude for how they enhanced your life.

After going through a loss, reminiscing about memories, even happy ones, can be difficult and distressing. It requires effort to let go of the emotions that come with recalling the memory. But by articulating what they meant to you in words, you may preserve those memories close to your heart forever.

Personal Reflections

Find your tranquil sanctuary, a place free from interruptions. Prepare to delve into the following thoughts - close your eyes, take a calming breath...and let your writing journey begin.

Dear _____, you meant the world to me, during our shared moments, you made me feel...

Dear _____, your laughter, which still echoes in my mind, always made me...

Dear _____, I realize that you taught me...

_____
_____
_____
_____
_____
_____
_____
_____
_____
_____
_____
_____
_____
_____

As you conclude this letter, you are reminded of the strength of your bond, a connection that transcends physical presence. You are comforted by our shared love and memories.

_____, Until we meet again in my next letter, know you are forever in my heart.

PLEASE USE YOUR JOURNAL TO WRITE DOWN INTUITIVE PROMPTS

Before concluding, kindly take a moment...

I often think about what I would do differently with my loved one if I had the chance. One of my favorite ideas is...

_____
_____
_____
_____
_____
_____
_____
_____

One thing I want to remember about you, one thing that I hold dear in my heart is...

_____
_____
_____
_____
_____
_____
_____
_____

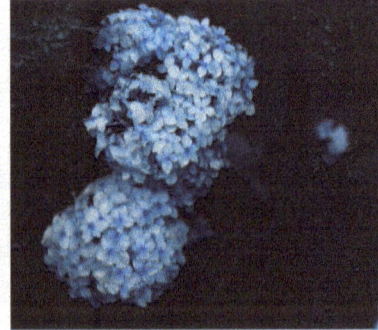

Take a breath in between. If you need to write more, please feel free to do so. Please write as many letters as you need to move your feelings into a space of peace within; I hope you got this...

LESSON 6   *Eliminated Grief*

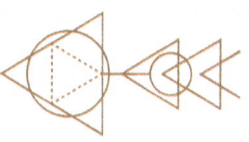

Over the past five lessons, you have expressed your loss in many ways. However, we have yet to discuss how loss manifests in the body. We have spoken about the link between body, mind, heart, and soul – each being as important as the other. If a loss impacts the reason, it also affects the other three. Therefore, caring for all parts of yourself is essential to maintaining a healthy lifestyle.

Typically, when people are asked to depict loss in the body, they may draw a broken heart, even though they understand that it's not physically torn. This illustrates how grief feels – like a sudden shock to the mind, confusion in the spirit, and pain in the heart. It's as if something crucial is missing from the body, creating a space in the heart.

In the past, if someone had mentioned feeling a hole in their heart due to loss, a doctor might have dismissed it as a mental issue. However, mind-body medicine has evolved significantly over the last two decades, as demonstrated by the phenomenon of ghost limbs, where amputees feel sensations in limbs they lost long ago. We now understand that the mind and body are intricately interconnected.

This can be linked to how the human heart misses a loved one. This "broken heart" feeling is more than just a metaphor. The emotional pain and stress that come with grief can trigger various physical symptoms, including chest pain, shortness of breath, and even changes in heart rhythm. This is due to the body's physiological response to intense emotions, potentially leading to a condition known as "broken heart syndrome" or Takotsubo cardiomyopathy.

Love is always connected to the heart; therefore, it is vulnerable when dealing with the loss of love. In a scientific sense, psychological responses are examples of the mind-body connection.

Not addressing grief can lead to serious conditions like depression and a lack of energy. That's why the 7 Stages of Grief were created with love and purpose.

Listen To Your Body:

Imagine your body as a vessel, a storyteller, whispering tales of your experiences, joys, and sorrows. When navigating the turbulent seas of grief, your body often becomes a lighthouse, signaling distress in its unique language. Writing, my dear reader, becomes a bridge, a translator, between you and your body's silent whispers. It's a proven salve, a balm that soothes the wounds of the heart, mind, and body.

Loss, you see, doesn't always echo in the heart's chambers. It can ripple out, touching every cell and every fiber of your being. It can sneak into your immune system, the body's fortress, and weaken defenses. Stress, the shadow of grief, can leave you vulnerable, especially if you're already grappling with health issues. Sometimes, it might even unmask a hidden ailment—a secret your body has kept.

Now, I don't mean to alarm you but rather to awaken you to the wisdom of your body. To help you understand its signals, listen to its stories.

Once you decipher how grief has etched itself into your physical being, you can start expressing it and releasing the pain. Writing about this pain can pave the path to healing and connection, regardless of distance.

So, let's embark on this journey together, pen in hand, ready to listen to our bodies' stories.

Message in a Bottle

Your body is a vessel carrying messages from your heart. It's like a bottle floating in the sea of your emotions, filled with words unsaid, feelings unfelt.

What physical sensations or changes have you noticed since your loss?

Write a letter to your loved one, sharing these observations as if they were messages in a bottle, cast into the sea of your shared memories.

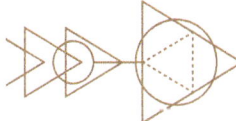

Stress, the shadow of grief, can leave imprints on your body. It's as if each wave of grief etches a message onto the bottle of your body.

How has stress manifested in your physical well-being? In your letter, describe these manifestations as messages etched onto a bottle, waiting to be discovered and understood.

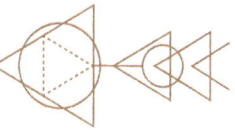

Writing about your pain can pave the path to healing, like a message in a bottle reaching your loved one.

What healing messages would you want to send to your loved one about your journey through grief? In your letter, imagine placing these healing messages into a bottle, letting them float across the sea of time and space to reach your loved one.

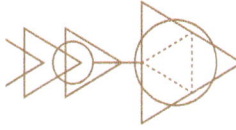

Write down whatever comes to mind without analyzing. Just let the pain speak for itself. Be Present with the physical connection to your grief as you write.

PLEASE USE YOUR JOURNAL TO WRITE YOUR THOUGHTS AND MESSAGES

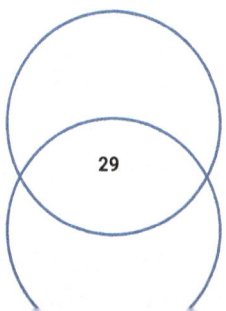

As we draw this chapter to a close, I invite you to pause and reflect on the following three questions

What emotions surfaced as you wrote your 'message in a bottle' to your loved one?

_____
_____
_____
_____
_____
_____

How has this exercise of writing letters to your loved one influenced your perspective on your grief journey?

_____
_____
_____
_____
_____
_____

What is one thing you learned about yourself through this process that you weren't aware of before?

_____
_____
_____
_____
_____
_____

If you feel the urge to write more, go ahead. Expressing your physical discomfort can bring relief and help you tune into your body's signals. Pay attention to what your body tells you and address concerns quickly to enhance your recovery. Treating your body with kindness and attentiveness is a vital part of self-care.

LESSON 7

Taking Notices *of* Coincidences

Let's discuss the mysterious realm beyond the veil, invisible to us but where departed loved ones reside. Even though we cannot see them, we can still sense their presence. When we put our feelings of loss into words, we create a heartfelt and enduring memorial. Grief is a complex emotion that grows without a cure. It goes beyond the limits of the body and the mind, hitting our very essence at the level of the soul and the heart.

EXPRESS is a philosophy that promotes candid discussions about death and dying. While it cannot eliminate the anguish of losing a loved one, it helps reduce the shame, fear, confusion, and stigma associated with grief. It is possible to find significance in our suffering.

I want you to throw yourself headfirst into this writing process. Give your mind permission to wander aimlessly into the unknown. If you keep digging, you might find something that helps you feel better. Keep an open mind and rely on your instincts. Do what is right for you, following your moral compass.

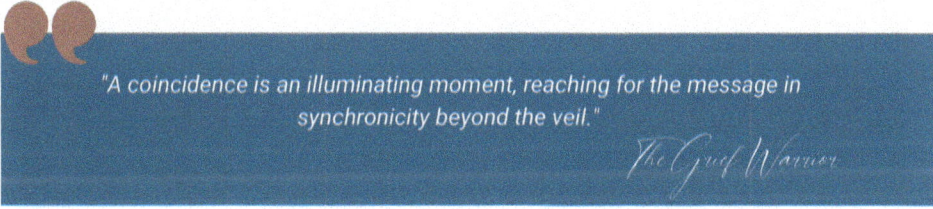

"A coincidence is an illuminating moment, reaching for the message in synchronicity beyond the veil."

The Grief Warrior

Embracing the Heart's Vision

Your mind, while powerful, is not the sole healer in times of loss. Logic alone cannot foster the connection you seek with your departed loved ones. The manner of their presence may remain a mystery, but their appearance in your life is a certainty. Writing letters to them can be a profound way to sense their enduring presence. Surrender to the longing for connection and remain receptive.

Beyond the Veil: Continuing the Conversation

Even in their absence, your loved ones can communicate their closeness to you. This communication can manifest in myriad ways, but there are certain consistent signs that you can trust, provided you are open to receiving and ready to embrace these messages from beyond the veil.

Sensing their Presence

The Physical Connection: You may experience a physical reaction, such as the hairs on your neck standing on end, signaling their closeness. Have faith in your inner knowing to identify these times, decipher the context, and know when they are near.

Serendipity: The Power of Happenstance

In the grand scheme of things, timing and location are everything. It likely is if an occurrence feels like an encounter with a departed loved one. If anything feels like meeting a dead relative, it probably is. Examples include seeing a prophetic sign at a loved one's funeral or running into a poignant reminder on a major anniversary. Sometimes, these deeply personal and perfectly timed signs are too profound to overlook. Rather than trying to orchestrate these happy coincidences, allow yourself to appreciate them when they organically unfold.

Here are some of the most common ones that people experience:

LIGHT

*Illuminated Memories:
Light in the Shadows of Loss.
Peculiar lights or orbs in photos or flickering of lights.*

BUTTERFLY

A symbol of metamorphosis is when the spirit leaves the body. This transformation is not an ending but a transition - a change in state rather than a cessation.

DREAMS

Comfort in Slumber's Embrace: Nocturnal encounters can provide solace, healing, and a sense of continued connection.

RAINBOWS

Serendipitous Sightings: Love's enduring symbols.

SOUND

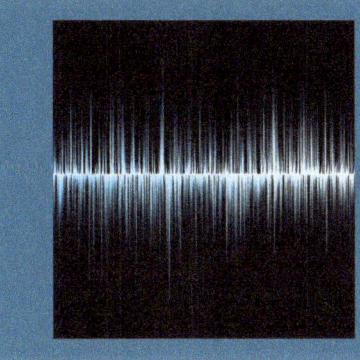

Echoes of the Heart: Voices and melodies from beyond.

ANIMALS

Feathered Messengers: Birds as symbols of hope and positivity.

TOUCH

The Unseen Embrace: A mysterious touch from a loved one.

OBJECTS

It is finding an item that feels like it was put there by your loved one.

SMELLS

Your loved one's natural smell, a fragrance they used to wear, and their favorite flower are all common signs.

Observing the experiences of others who have gone through a similar loss can be beneficial to gain insight into what may be possible for your own healing journey. Try using theta meditation first thing in the morning to train your mind to be open and accepting.

Be accepting of yourself and others as you recover. Positive developments can show themselves in various ways, some more noticeable than others. The recovery process can be tremendously aided by maintaining awareness and openness to these shifts.

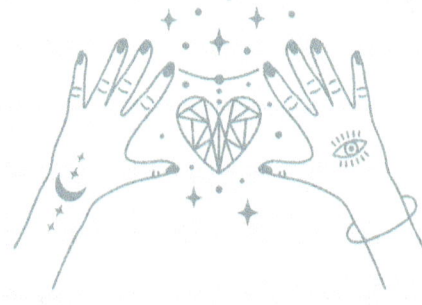

Heart2Heart

Try penning a letter to yourself—just not from your own point of view. Try writing it from your loved one's point of view instead. Allow their words of love and encouragement to flow from their heart through your fingertips and onto paper.

What do they think they'd say? Can you imagine any words of solace or support they might say? How would they constantly remind you of your undying love for one another?

This is not an opportunity for fantasy or wishful thinking. It's a method to reconnect with the unconditional love that your departed friend or family member gave you. So let this letter represent their words, a symbol of their love, and a reminder of the strength of your relationship.

Dear (Your Name), If your loved one did anything to inspire you, what was it?

_____
_____
_____
_____
_____
_____
_____
_____
_____
_____
_____
_____
_____
_____

Put your reaction and feelings into words as best you can. Write from the heart and be authentic. Let your loved one know everything you have to express.

**Before you conclude this heartfelt exercise, pause and reflect.
Ask yourself these soul-searching questions:**

What are the unique qualities, gestures, or moments that you deeply miss about your loved one?

_____
_____
_____
_____
_____
_____

Is there a recent event, a milestone, or a simple everyday occurrence you wish to share with them?

_____
_____
_____
_____
_____
_____

Have you recently noticed coincidences that remind you of your loved one? Please elaborate.

_____
_____
_____
_____
_____
_____

PLEASE USE YOUR JOURNAL TO WRITE DOWN YOUR THOUGHTS

LESSON 8

A Message *from* Your Loved One

This is a sacred space where we'll explore the profound and mysterious ways our departed loved ones still speak to us.

Could our loved ones communicate with us through an unbreakable cord of love that transcends death?

Listen with an open heart for messages from loved ones who have crossed over to the other side, *beyond the veil*. They want to be heard; all we have to do is *pay attention*.

Voices Beyond the Veil: Understanding Messages from Loved Ones

In the quiet corners of our everyday lives, there exists a gentle hum, a whispering echo that resonates from a world beyond our own. These are the dimensions from which our departed loved ones communicate with us.

Imagine a familiar tune playing when you're thinking of them or a vivid dream that feels like a visit. These aren't mere coincidences but meaningful messages from beyond the veil.

These moments, these messages, are not mere figments of our imagination. They are tangible signs from our loved ones, assuring us of their continued existence in different forms and dimensions. These transmissions can be as brief as a butterfly's wingbeat or as soft as a feather's touch. In our dreams, our departed loved ones can visit us, their words and deeds as meaningful and kind as they were in life.

You will learn to trust and trust these clues along the way. You will learn how our loved ones reach out to us, providing comfort, love, and the certainty that the physical world does not bind the bond.

Let's journey together, listening to the whispers of the unseen. The limitless strength of love will be on full display for all to see. We will explore the peace and security of knowing loved ones are never far away.

The Inner Voice

The Inner Voice echoes the presence of our loved ones. This lesson is a testament to the power of memory and the enduring bonds of love that transcends physical presence.

To prepare for this task, gather items that remind you of your loved one. This could be photographs, letters, artwork, or any object that holds a special significance. Spend time with these items, let them stir your memories, and awaken the senses connecting you to your loved one.

Take a moment to immerse yourself in these reminders. Try to recall the sounds of their laughter, the scent that was uniquely theirs, the warmth of their touch, or the comfort of their presence.

Now, bring these items where you feel comfortable and ready to write. Let these objects serve as silent conversationalists, their energy contributing to the narrative you're about to weave. Creating an altar will enhance the power to receive...

Let "The Inner Voice" guide your words as you write in this lesson. This voice imbued with the essence of your loved one, will lend authenticity to your writing. Remember, the more your writing resonates with their voice, the more healing the process will be.

Postcards to the Stars: Expressing What Can't Be Said

This is your opportunity to articulate those sentiments that have yet to be voiced, to bridge the gap between the here and the beyond. Before your pen touches the paper, close your eyes.

Visualize your loved one. Recall the sound of their laughter, the warmth of their gaze, the comfort of their presence. Hold these memories close as you prepare to write.

Launch into your letter. Let the words pour out of you as you write their name, evoking their very being on the page. Share with them the moments of your life they've missed, the dreams you're chasing, the struggles you're encountering.

Express those unvoiced sentiments. Maybe it's a birthday greeting you forgot to send, an apology you had to postpone, or just a declaration of your undying love. Fill your "Postcard to the Stars" using these words.

Once you have finished writing your letter, you may just read it out loud. Allow your words to fill the room, giving your loved one's memory a place to flourish.

Remember, this is your letter, your connection to your loved one. There's no right or wrong way to do this. It's about giving voice to your heart's unspoken words, about keeping the bond alive, even across the stars.

As you conclude this exercise, gently ponder over these two questions.

What emotions surfaced as you penned this letter? Reflect on their role in your healing journey.

_____
_____
_____
_____
_____
_____
_____
_____

Did writing this letter bring any sense of relief or closure? Consider its impact on your journey toward peace.

_____
_____
_____
_____
_____
_____
_____
_____

PLEASE USE YOUR JOURNAL TO EXPRESS THESE THOUGHTS

Feel free to continue writing if you have more to say. You can even revisit your previous letters and respond to them if it feels appropriate. Stay open-minded and allow yourself to fully immerse in this experience. Consider creating a ritual to release any negative emotions and listen to your inner voice.

LESSON 9

The Burning Letter Ritual *for* Release

I love the use of rituals. Rituals cause us to take pause, giving weight to things that are significant to us. Rituals help us concentrate, stay present, and provide a sense of emotional and spiritual grounding. One such ritual that has been used historically for release is burning.

Nothing is more disruptive than the death of someone you love who intertwines with your being. When those people die, we are left floundering. The degree of connection you had with the deceased, whether spiritual, emotional, or physical, and how you view your existence both impact how intense your grief is. The stronger the bond you share, the more profound the impact of their death on your grieving process.

On my son's 36th birthday, memories flooded my mind as I embarked on a poignant ritual. It had been 17 years since he transitioned, and I felt compelled to let go of the weight that had clung to my heart. In the tranquil surroundings of my ancestral home, I set up a cauldron borrowed from my kitchen, ready to burn the remnants of the past. Sipping champagne, I settled on the grass, watching as the flames danced in hues of purple and yellow. With each funeral memento, I fed into the fire, my heavy heart became fleeting. These moments of emotional liberation held profound significance on my journey, nourishing the depths of my inner being.

Find a photograph of your loved one, place it before you, and light a candle. As you gaze into the flame, envision it as an illuminating guide for them to come to you. It is powerful to embrace your feelings, summon your memories, and invite them into your space.

The Palo Santo is burned before the ritual to purify the surroundings. You can use a fireproof bowl chosen explicitly for the burning ceremony, which holds sentimental value, or any vessel you already own—performing the ritual in a serene location where you can sit undisturbed, preferably outdoors in nature.

Full Moon Ritual

It's important to feel comfortable reading out loud.
The point is to read the letter out loud to your loved one to sense a connection. Why does this matter? When you read aloud, you fill your voice with energy, express your feelings through your words, and give them life. Take your time to facilitate emotional healing. If you're feeling overwhelmed, give yourself some time to recover. Feel free to express your feelings, whether tears of joy or laughter to the sky. If you're feeling overwhelmed, give yourself some time to recover. Don't be afraid to show your emotions by crying tears of joy or laughing until you hurt.

Prepare yourself to release your loved one to the universe.
Once you have read your letter aloud, hold it close to you. Take some time to reflect on what you have read and cherish the memories. When ready, hold the letter out and release your loved one by saying, "I release [name of a loved one] and their energy from my life. I am grateful for the time we spent together. With love, I release with gratitude. I release with love. I will release you to the universe and begin my healing journey."

Embracing Release: A Ritual of Purging and Remembrance
First, while holding the letter, fold it away from you to "let go" of the contents. Then, fold the letter outward as if presenting it as an offering to the infinite space of the universe. Turn the letter counterclockwise three times to imbue it with a spirit of letting go. Put the letter inside a fireproof container and light it with care. Watch in silence as the fire consumes the letter. Allow happy memories of your loved one to arise at this sacred time, welcoming the cleansing process with open arms.

Honoring the Ashes: A Choice of Resting Place
Once the letter has been transformed into ashes, a decision awaits on how to honor their presence. You can scatter the ashes in a cherished corner of your yard, allowing them to blend with the earth. Alternatively, you may bury them, providing a permanent resting place. Another possibility is to release the ashes to the whims of the wind, allowing nature to guide their dispersal. If you feel compelled to keep the ashes, they can be saved in an urn until the perfect location for scattering or safekeeping reveals itself. The choice is yours, guided by your profound connection with your loved one.

Reverent Cleansing of the Fireproof Bowl
It is time to pay attention to the fireproof bowl holding the transformative flames. Approach this task with intention, taking your time to ensure thorough cleansing. Let it symbolize closure and renewal, preparing the fireproof bowl for future journeys of remembrance and catharsis.

Filling the Void with Positive Energy
Choose a mantra that resonates deeply with you and invokes positive emotions and associations. Visualize this chosen mantra as an inspiration of positive energy, drawing it into the void left behind by grief.

Liberation Unveiled: A Full Moon Letter of Release and Renewal

As the full moon graces the night sky, we invite you to embark on a transformative journey of realization and letting go. Let us begin this ritual with a proud bow to your unwavering courage.

Dear _____,

Writing this letter has triggered a flood of wonderful memories from our time together. I can still feel your presence, influencing my actions and inspiring my feelings. Pieces of our shared joy and love are woven together in my heart like a beautiful tapestry. My heart is heavy, but I am grateful for the time we shared; therefore, I am writing down my love, thankfulness, and gratitude for you.

In the depths of remembrance, I discover a wellspring of strength. Even in your absence, your grace remains a source of inspiration. As I navigate this path of recollection, I lovingly ask for your gentle guidance. Help me move forward with reverence, carrying the essence of our connection in every step I take.

With love and gratitude,

_____

WRITE THIS LETTER INTO YOUR JOURNAL

Feel free to continue writing if you have more to say. You can even revisit your previous letters and respond to them if it feels appropriate. Stay open-minded and allow yourself to fully immerse in this experience. Consider creating a ritual to release any negative emotions and listen to your inner voice.

In the tapestry of life, the grief journey tells a captivating tale, where *love and strength* emerge as the resilient threads that mend the heart.

The Grief Warrior

LESSON 10

The Power of Connection and Healing

Reflecting on the Journey

Now that the course has concluded, a new chapter unfolds in your journey of healing and connection with your lost loved one. As we reflect on the transformative path we've walked together, let us delve into the significance of time and its profound impact on our well-being. It is often said that time can heal all things, but we have learned that time alone is not enough. Intentionally investing time in healing and self-care can expedite healing and transformation.

In this final chapter, I invite you to engage in an interactive closing engagement, where we will explore a series of questions and prompts to deepen your connection with your loved one and foster healing in your life. By taking these deliberate steps towards communication and healing, we hope this journey has been helpful and profoundly meaningful to your life.

How would you describe your heart and emotions when you first started?

- How has this course impacted your understanding of grief and loss?
- What are some key insights or realizations you have gained along the way?
- Share a specific moment or exercise that significantly impacted your healing process.

How have your beliefs served you when you first started? And now?

- What steps will you take to initiate communication with your loved one?
- How do you envision these conversations or connections unfolding?
- Are there any specific messages or sentiments you wish to EXPRESS?

How are you doing mentally in the present day? Do you feel lighter?

- What self-care practices or rituals will you prioritize to support your healing journey?
- How can you create a safe and nurturing space for yourself to process your emotions?
- Are there any additional resources or support systems you plan to explore?

Have you noticed any healing or growth in your heart and emotional well-being?

- Reflect on the shifts and changes you have experienced since the beginning of this journey.
- Are there specific practices or moments contributing to this feeling of lightness?

Integration and Moving Forward:

- How do you plan to integrate the lessons and insights gained from this course into your daily life?
- What actions or changes are you inspired to make to live a more meaningful and fulfilling life?
- In what ways will you carry the memories and essence of your lost loved one as you move forward?

As you engage with these questions and prompts, trust in the wisdom within you. This closing engagement is an opportunity for introspection, growth, and intention setting. Remember, this is not the end but a continuation of your journey toward healing and connection.

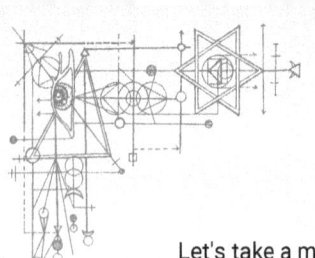

Let's take a moment to reflect on the first lesson and the experience of writing your first letter about a positive memory. Recall the emotions and sensations that arose as you put pen to paper and allowed the words to flow.

What was your favorite letter and why?
- Reflect on the various letters you have written since the beginning of this journey.
- Consider which letter resonated with you the most or made a deep connection.

How did your favorite letter make you feel?
- Describe the emotions and sensations that emerged as you crafted this letter.
- Did it evoke a profound sense of joy, healing, or nostalgia?
- Explore the impact this letter had on your overall well-being and inner state.

How did writing contribute to any changes in your memories?
- Describe the effects of writing on your overall recollection and interpretation of the past.
- Consider how introspection and putting thoughts into words impacted your understanding.

Have these changes in your memories brought about any shifts in your emotional well-being?
- Explore the connection between the evolving nature of your memories and your emotional state.
- Reflect on any emotional transformations that have occurred as a result of writing about your memories.

Did you learn anything new about your relationship with your loved one?
- Reflect on the letters and reflections you have written throughout this journey.
- Explore any newfound understanding of the dynamics, emotions, or aspects of your connection with your loved one.

Did writing help you set boundaries with family or friends?
- Reflect on your writing journey and the topics you have explored.
- Explore whether writing provided clarity, assertiveness, or a sense of empowerment in setting boundaries.

Did you feel the one you lost was close at any point?
- Reflect on your experiences throughout the ritual writing.
- Recall moments when you sensed the presence or connection of your loved one.

How did you know that the one you lost was close?
- Describe the specific cues, experiences, or intuitions that made you feel their presence.
- Did you notice any synchronicities, vivid dreams, or unexplainable occurrences that evoked a sense of their closeness?

If you had the opportunity to ask your loved one who has passed away one last question, what would it be, and why is it important to you?

Through this transformative journey, you have granted yourself the invaluable gift of time and space to heal and reconnect with what you have lost. You have navigated the depths of pain and emptiness, emerging stronger and wiser. Your letters have woven a powerful narrative of love, loss, and healing, a testament to your resilience and courage. The strength of the written word, the breadth of your imagination, and the enduring force of love have propelled you forward with each pen stroke as you begin the next chapter of your life. Your journey is truly inspiring.

"Our sorrows and wounds are healed only when we touch them with compassion."

Buddha

With heartfelt wishes for your continued growth and fulfillment, I am grateful for holding your heart on this transformative exploration. May the lessons embrace and the connections enrich your life, and may you find solace and healing in the profound power of love and remembrance.

I want you to know how much I appreciate your strength and perseverance as we close this chapter.

Writing Homework

Find your usual spot, embracing the stillness surrounding your rejuvenated spirit as you embark on this final letter with reverence and reflection.

My dearest (loved one), it has truly been an amazing journey. From the moment I wrote that very first letter, I never could have imagined...

_____
_____
_____
_____
_____
_____
_____
_____
_____

Beloved Warriors,

As you have journeyed through our first stage, EXPRESS, I am reminded of the strength we endure each day. In your commitment to this exploration, you display courage — of inner quests. Each emotion and story written is a chapter in the grand narrative you're weaving.

The EMBRACE framework is a humble guide towards healing, understanding, and illuminating the way for yourself and others.

"In seeking, we often find in healing ourselves, we light the way for others."

With Healing Intentions, MiMi

MEDITATE
The Second Stage of Grief

EMBRACE

MICHELE C. BELL
THE GRIEF WARRIOR®

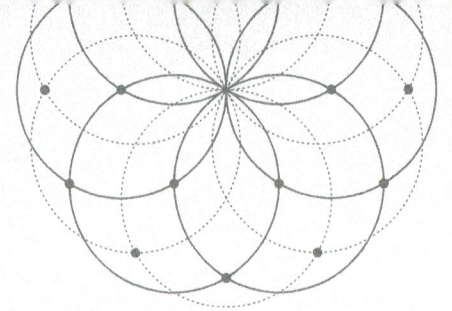

you've made it

You are now ready to **EMBRACE** our Second Stage:

That's the blessing and power of **pivoting with purpose.**

What are the 7 Stages of Grief Alignment?
Express. **M**editate.
Be Present. **R**ejuvenate.
Awaken. **C**onnect. **E**at Healthy.

Healing begins with acceptance, and alignment transforms us through embracing our circumstances.

The empowerment of embracing is in your next chapter – are you ready to turn the page?

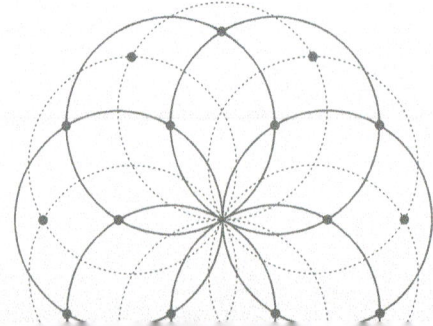

Table of Contents

Meditation 101:
How Will Meditation Guide Your Journey? 03

Trauma and Meditation: Hurting, Healing, & Hope 09

The Stages of Grief Alignment 15

Four Ways to Heal: Cultivate Positivity, Enrich it,
Absorb it, and Correlate Positivity & Negativity 22

Creating a Meditation Space for Healing 27

Healing in Action: Meditation Exercise for Trauma 33

Meditation Techniques to Transition
Purposefully Using the Body Scan Method 38

Rituals for Remembrance:
Rite of Passage Moon Meditation 45

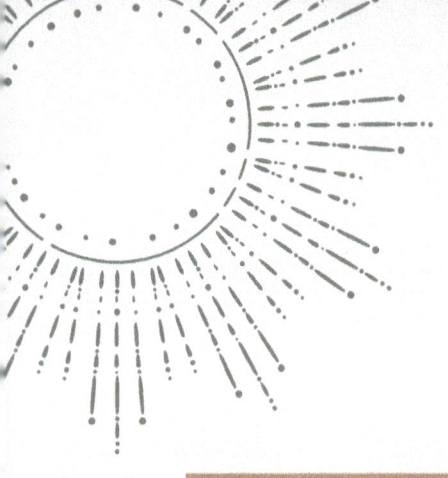

Meditation 101:
How Will Meditation Guide Your Journey?

Objective: To understand the benefits of meditation and how you can access it as a tool in your journey toward healing.

Ignite Your Warrior Spirit

Grand Rising Warriors, allow me to be your trusted guide on this next exciting chapter of your journey as you EMBRACE the possibilities. Together, we will explore, learn, and grow, allowing it all to shape us into courageous leaders with a greater understanding of our true selves!

Even when life seems overwhelming, there is still a way out. Meditation can release our burdens—anxieties, stress, memories, and trauma. By taking moments to breathe deeply, ask for assistance, and find peace in letting go, meditation allows us to refocus on what matters most: ourselves.

Why Meditation?

Since the beginning of time, humanity has sought to understand and harmonize with its internal energies through meditation. By clearing our minds of woes, we can journey towards gracefully handling external burdens - allowing us to transcend into spiritual enlightenment.

Meditation serves as a guiding light, illuminating the path to relaxation and stress relief and redirecting our focus toward the positive. It tunes us into the harmonious symphony of our inner universe, fostering a profound connection that exudes calmness and joy in our interactions with ourselves and others.

In mindfulness meditation, we step away from the chaos of our hectic lifestyles, entering a sphere of consciousness that invites relaxation, refocusing, and genuine reflection.

Meditation is a beautiful journey of self-discovery. We take time to get in touch with our innermost thoughts, feelings, and sensations without judgment or expectation. In doing so, we can transcend the stresses of day-to-day life and tap into an infinite source of peace within ourselves.

By living in the present moment, embracing silence as our trusted companion, radiating our inner light outwardly, and releasing all that obstructs our path to happiness, true healing, and contentment await us.

The Healing Benefits of Meditation

Many practitioners, coaches, and gurus have probably told you that meditation is a powerful tool for personal growth and healing.

This is a perfect example of the lovely intersection of magic and science. Here are some of the well-documented advantages that meditation can bring to your journey:

- Manage anxiety, depression, and stress (the portion of the brain responsible for regulating pressure and anxiety can shrink by regularly practicing meditation!)

- Improve your overall mood and well-being.

- You can connect with your inner self.

- Comprehend the traumas of the past and move towards your future.

- Instant sensations of healing and relief.

- Better sleep and rest.

- Sharpen your short- and long-term memory.

- You can increase your focus.

- You can explore your creative instincts.

- Improve your cognitive and problem-solving abilities.

- Support your efforts to break free from addiction by maintaining self-control.

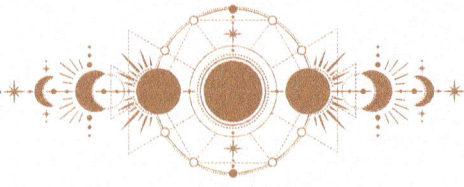

Why Will Meditation Help YOU?

- If you're here, you may be hurting.

- Maybe you've lost a child. A sibling. A friend. A loved one. Your reality feels shattered, and you're left to pick up the pieces.

- Know you're not alone in this. This pain might not go away forever, but your strength and ability to grieve and carry it in grace can empower you to move forward.

- That throughout all this pain, you can pivot with purpose. To embrace, to empower.

- It starts by looking within and honoring your emotions, learning to sit with them, and encouraging your resilience to breathe through grief, heartache, and sorrow.

- To break toxic cycles, shift your focus to the present and show yourself the gratitude, love, and care you deserve.

- It all starts with just a few meditative moments each day. Let's choose you and heal you.

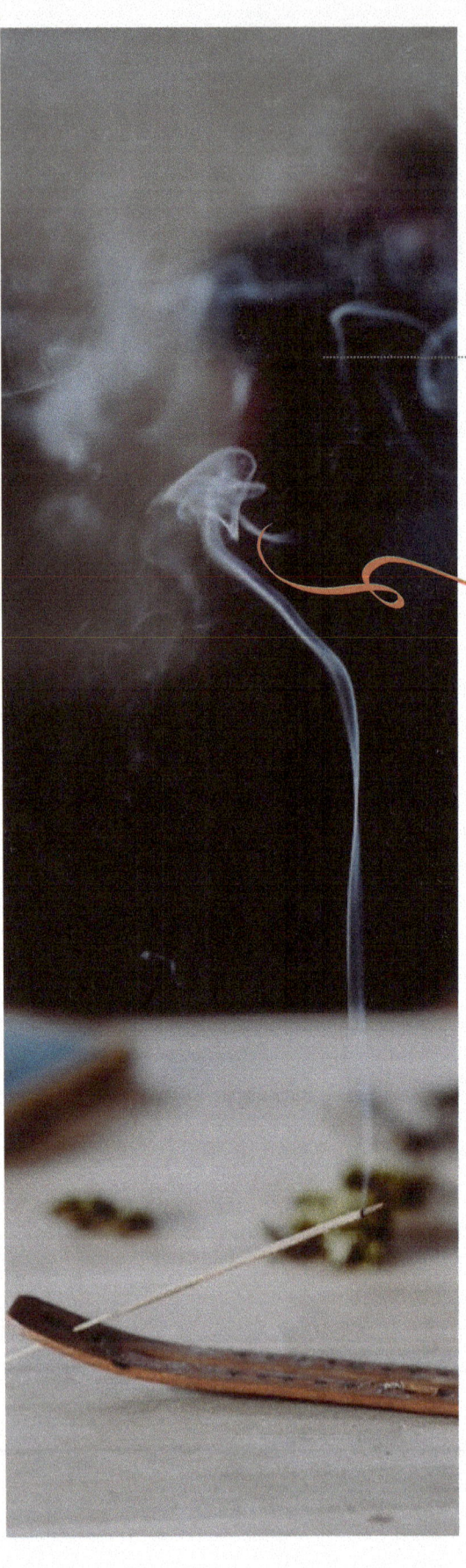

Key Points

- Meditation can help us carry and release heavy emotions, difficult memories, and traumatic experiences.

- It allows us to unwind, quiet our minds, and become at ease with the unpleasant.

- Benefits: Manage anxiety, depression, and stress; improve mood; connect with your inner self; process trauma; get instant relief; get better sleep; sharpen memory; improve focus; access creativity; improve cognition; and increase self-control.

Exercise

As we go through each chapter, please envision yourself beginning and concluding a new chapter on your journey. At the end of each chapter, I will lead you through a straightforward yet effective meditation exercise to provide immediate relief and spark your healing process.

To practice an Earthing meditation, kindly follow the instructions below:

Earthing, or grounding, is a form of meditation that can balance your energy and connect you with Mother Nature to find peace in the present moment.

It's simple: Connect with the Earth.

Try this exercise today. Find a serene location where you can unwind and relax without shoes, such as a grassy backyard or park with natural elements like dirt or rocks. Enjoy the grounding sensation and embrace the present moment.

 Be mindful of each step, walking slowly and mindfully: How does the earth feel on your skin?

 Take off your shoes and walk on the earth.

 Synchronize your breath with each step. Focus only on your breath and sensations.

 If your mind wanders, no worries. Gently shift your focus back to your breath and the earth.

 Do this for as long or as little as you please. Toward the end, express gratitude to yourself for taking the time to practice grounding.

 Now, express gratitude to the Earth and your Creator for offering you this moment of healing and beauty.

Trauma and Meditation:
Hurting, Healing, & Hope

Objective: To validate the mental and physical impact, the relationship between mindfulness and trauma, and how to let go of painful memories using meditation.

The Mental & Physical Manifestation of Loss

While death is the opposite of life, it is an inevitable part of it. And for some of us, we know the traumatic reality far sooner than we ever thought.

The feeling can be overwhelming and intense, whether it is the loss of a friend, parent, sibling, or spouse. From profound sadness to depression, shock, numbness, guilt, regret, or emptiness, the grief experience is a tumultuous sea of heavy emotions that are difficult to bear. You might even feel angry at yourself, your family, a loved one, or God. Maybe you've noticed behaviors that didn't feel right to you:

- Excessive alertness
- Continuous crying
- Avoiding social gatherings and interaction with people An urge to harm yourself
- Avoidance
- The inclination toward alcohol and substance abuse

If this is what you're feeling or experiencing, please know you're not alone. Your feelings are valid. Your experience is authentic, raw, and sometimes ruthless. And while the emotions you're carrying may seem too heavy to lift on your own, know there is hope. You are stronger than you know; life might not seem the same again, but you must focus on the future with hope and optimism to move forward.

Your health, personality, and support can strengthen you to carry your grief and move forward in growth. To pivot with purpose and embrace what's ahead of you while still honoring what's behind you.

The Philosophy of Mindfulness & Trauma

In our dance through life, the delicate art of looking forward while casting a glance back lends our journey its depth. Each soul bears the imprints of trauma differently, reminding us of the individuality of our human experience. Drawing from ancient traditions, we've turned to meditation as a profound wellspring of healing for both heart and mind.

Mindfulness is a steadfast companion in our journey through the maze of grief. It signals us not with loud proclamations but with a gentle invitation to be present and acknowledge our past's wounds. Through daily immersion in meditative reflection, we create sanctuaries of calm, pockets of peace in which our souls find rest. This awakened consciousness becomes our shield and guide, helping us cherish memories of our departed while finding the strength to continue our journey.

Healing is, in essence, a pilgrimage towards understanding our stormy seas of emotions. Instead of fleeing, facing them allows us to chart a path through the depths of our past pain toward the promise of tomorrow. In this raw vulnerability and sincere pursuit, we find the seeds of true recovery, promising us a journey filled with hope and brighter tomorrows.

Letting Go of the Pain & Pivoting with Purpose

Loss isn't only felt through the departure of loved ones. Whether parting from a beloved pet, confronting unmet dreams, or saying farewell to a former home, every situation brings unique heartache that we often sweep under the rug. *Have you ever caught yourself minimizing a pain simply because it wasn't about the loss of a person? How did that make you feel?*

Yet, by confronting this pain, we find solace and allow these memories to enrich our grasp of life's profound teachings. *Can you recall when confronting a painful memory brought you unexpected peace or understanding?*

Navigating the intense emotions that follow a significant loss is a challenge. We seek wholesome ways to cope, transcend anguish, and rediscover life's purpose. *What coping strategies have you tried in the past, and which ones felt most genuine to your healing process?*

By immersing ourselves in meditation and mindfulness, we can accept our painful recollections and find healing. This deliberate path calls for dedication, assisting us in reconciling with our losses and seeking avenues for renewed growth. *Do you find solace in stillness and introspection, or does it feel daunting to confront your feelings head-on?*

Moving With, as we let go of what once was and channel our experiences into purpose, we gain clarity. *How has an experience shaped your present purpose or perspective?*

Key Points

- Grief and loss are unique personal experiences that can provoke intense mental, emotional, and physical manifestations.

- Your health, personality, and support can strengthen you to carry your grief and move forward in growth.

- Meditation has always been integral to healing from the trauma of the unexpected loss of a loved one.

- You can come to terms with your loss with time and conscious efforts.

 # Exercise

Before we start this next exercise together, I want you to be gentle with yourself. Meditation and mindfulness can surface intense memories and emotions, allowing us to work through them and begin our healing journeys. However, if you experience PTSD or painful flashbacks and symptoms, please take a step back, give yourself space, and reach out for help. Our goal is to help you feel safe, mindful, and strong.

You've got this. Follow the prompts below to get started.

01 Find a private, peaceful place to sit comfortably for 10-15 minutes.

02 Get comfortable – you can use pillows, blankets, or other comfort items.

03 Take a deep breath in slowly.

04 Inhale for 5 seconds.

05 Hold for 5 seconds.

06 Exhale for 5 seconds.

07 Repeat five times.

08 Now, shift your breath to your body and mind. Check-in with yourself. It is not good or bad. --realize how you're feeling from an outside perspective as if you were a loving friend or family member.

09 How is your body feeling? Give it compassion and grace.

Exercise

10. How is your mind feeling? Give it empathy and understanding.

11. Now, imagine the loved one you are grieving. Picture the happiest version of their face.

12. If you could say anything to them, think about it or say it aloud. Focus on healing and grace.

13. Now, imagine their response in a loving, kind way. Could you let it be the words you need to hear?

14. Now, let your mind drift into a visualization of a happy memory with them. Allow yourself to experience this memory in your mind entirely.

15. Once ready, shift your focus back to your breath.

16. Take a deep breath in slowly. Inhale for 5 seconds.

17. Hold for 5 seconds.

18. Exhale for 5 seconds.

19. Repeat five times.

20. Slowly open your eyes when ready and reflect on your experiences. Be gentle with yourself for the rest of the day.

The Stages of Grief & The Stages of Grief Alignment

> **Objective:** To understand the five stages of grief, how to heal through your grief using meditation, and move from acceptance to embracing.

The Journey of Grief

Grief. It's such a personal yet almost mysterious word. Even those sitting face-to-face with our grief rarely find the right words to describe it. Experts have whittled it down into a 5-step path to help us better understand this individual yet shared experience:

Five Stages of Grief

Together, we will focus more on the 7 Stages of Grief Alignment. But before we can embrace, we must first understand.

Here's a simple overview of the Five Stages of Grief:

1. Denial: No, this cannot be happening to me.
2. Anger—Why me? Who's blaming? I do not deserve this!
3. Bargaining: Don't do this. Do not, and I will _____!
4. Depression: Life is unfair to me. There is only darkness. I can't handle it anymore.
5. Acceptance: I accept this sudden and unfortunate turn in life. I am at peace with it.

I gently ask you to take a moment and think: Where are you on this journey?

Give yourself grace, as there is no wrong answer now. We can only move *with*, moving forward, pivoting with purpose to embrace the 7 stages of grief alignment.

The Journey of Healing

One of the core elements of healing from trauma is to discover, address, and work through it. Meditation is one of the most potent tools found within us that allows us to confront our grief and move forward with a renewed sense of freedom and love for ourselves and others. Through meditation, you can heal all your wounds and touch on each area of grief, trauma, bullying, and abuse. While it can challenge your mind and heart, meditation trains your awareness. It lets you control your thoughts and eliminate distractions that trigger emotional wandering and habitual negativity.

Whether through breathwork, journaling, or yoga, shifting our awareness to the here and now can allow us to make amends with our past and intentionally pave a healthy future. Reconsidering experiences from this newfound mindset will equip us with clarity to create healthy futures filled with purposeful intent! Take a moment to pause and observe. When you do, there is an opportunity for growth and healing. Accepting your feelings instead of denying them builds strength and courage that can fuel you forward.

Your Next Steps to Acceptance

- Recognize your grief or loss. Consider it from a distance and express empathy to yourself.

- Recognize that you may go through various and unexpected emotional changes.

- Recognize that each person's grief process is unique. There is no 'correct' way to mourn.

- Seek the help and support of others. Seek the advice of a mental health professional if necessary.

- Accept responsibility for your emotional, mental, and physical health.

The Seven Stages of Grief Alignment

While the Five Stages help us better understand our grief experience, the fifth stage isn't the final. It's the beginning of a new, intentional journey—the journey to embracing The 7 Stages of Grief Alignment saved me. They taught me to embrace, empower, and pivot from pain to purpose.

EXPRESS
Write all your emotions, your heavy feelings, without judgment. Release to find peace.

MEDITATE
Releasing and letting go. Find healing in intention. Open yourself up to the universe and connect your body, mind, and spirit to the healing power of the present moment—heavy feelings without judgment.

BE PRESENT
Stop keeping yourself busy and be still. Breathe in. Breathe out. Carve out moments to release the hustle and allow yourself to *be* in the **POD** - Pause. Observe. Discern.

REJUVENATE
Disconnect to reconnect. Whether going on trips and adventures with friends or reading a book in bed, self-care is sacred. Energize and rejuvenate your soul. Make time for your inner sanctuary. Take control; create moments of peace so you can fully reconnect!

AWAKEN
Practice mindfulness -- observe yourself from a higher, divine perspective. Tune into the PAUSE. Let go of the past and trust in the future. Enjoy the now.

CONNECT
Connect your mind, body, and spirit. Give gratitude, shift to the positive, and meditate on what gives you hope.

EAT HEALTHY
Food is fuel. I'm not saying you should follow a fad diet or restrict yourself. The goal of embracing is to become more in sync with your inner and higher selves. Listen to your body and give it the flavors, nutrients, and energy it needs. You don't have to do it all at once; we're just focused on meditation. Allow yourself to accept and embrace your healing journey, one step at a time.

Key Points

- To heal, you must first acknowledge your feelings. Accept them.

- While the Five Stages help us better understand our grief experience, the fifth stage isn't final. It's the beginning of a new, intentional journey –the journey to embracing.

- There's healing by tuning into your inner world, caring for yourself, and living in the present moment.

Exercise

For this chapter's exercise, we will combine the powers of our first two elements of EMBRACE: Express and Meditate. Answer the questions and follow the prompts below. BREATHE, PAUSE in between each moment, and feel all of it.

01 Find a journal and something to write with.

02 Now, permit yourself to express yourself.

03 Tell yourself that there is no judgment here.

04 Now, write all your emotions. Your heavy feelings. Imagine them releasing from your body as you write them down.

05 Be gentle with yourself through this process.

06 Once you've reached the end of your writing flow state, take a step back and breathe.

07 Close your eyes.

08 Breathe in for 5 seconds.

09 Hold for 5 seconds.

10 Breathe out for 5 seconds.

11 Repeat five times, focusing solely on your breath.

Exercise

12 Now, imagine you're observing yourself from outside of your body. Objectively keep the thoughts, emotions, and experiences you wrote.

13 Imagine observing these thoughts as the most loving, understanding person or creature you know. Maybe it's God, a loved one, or even a pet.

14 Imagine yourself as that being; give yourself that grace, nonjudgmental love, support, and embrace you seek.

15 Allow yourself to sit in the warmth and light of this love.

16 Once you're ready, shift your focus back to the present.

17 Breathe in for 5 seconds.

18 Hold for 5 seconds.

19 Breathe out for 5 seconds.

20 When you're ready, open your eyes.

Four Ways to Heal:
Cultivate Positivity, Enrich it, Absorb it, Correlate Positivity & Negativity

Objective: To learn how to use your energy and focus on healing your heart and spirit.

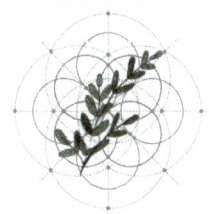

Cultivate Positivity

Our focus shapes our life experiences. By simply spending a moment to discuss the hue of yellow, we can suddenly realize how prevalent this vibrant color is in everyday life —it's not as if more objects have appeared out of thin air; instead, simply by changing how we look at things, new perspectives are a sight to embrace!

Now, this applies to positivity and negativity as well. If you focus on the positive, you'll see more light in your life. If you dwell on the negative, you'll see more shadows.

The journey toward recovery begins with cultivating a positive, uplifting mindset. However, this is far from an effortless endeavor, particularly for those who have suffered multiple traumas or are naturally inclined to look on the darker side of things.

Now is the time to take charge of your mindset by training your brain to appreciate all that's positive in life. Instead of searching far and wide, look closer than you think: it's already within reach! Tap into a feeling full of support and security; this will help bring more joyous experiences to your journey.

Through meditation, we can pause and catch glimpses of the ever-present divine support. Gratitude becomes easier to embody when we give ourselves space for stillness, allowing us to experience all the blessings this world has waiting for us.

Enrich it

It's easy to get bogged down with daily struggles, but what if we took the time to savor and relish our happy moments? Taking a few minutes each day to reflect on these positive memories can help revive your optimism! Try embracing even small, joyful experiences as an opportunity for growth.

Appreciate the beauty that life offers and savor each moment. Let your spirit soar when you receive a compliment, and document special occasions with photographs or memories so they will never be forgotten. Instead of dwelling on difficult times, meditate on your past's positive memories rather than ruminate on the painful ones. How might cherishing the good moments reshape your perspective on the challenges?

Absorb it

Immerse yourself in the bliss of unbridled joy, allowing it to seep into your spirit and touch every aspect of your being. Allow freedom, happiness, and optimism to become a permanent fixture within the depths of your heart—forever positive!

Allow the light of optimism to take away your sorrow and pain; healing heart harmony has brought that low. Embrace the positive facets of life; they'll cast an illuminating glow, fostering internal healing. How might your days change if you consistently nurtured this inner light?

Correlate Positivity & Negativity

Believe that change is calling your name; remove the bad influences from your life to make room for hope. Free yourself from burdens that don't cultivate a space for hope and positivity!

This can mean creating boundaries with people, places, and things that drain you rather than fuel you. Setting clear boundaries with what brings you down can help you release some of the weight of the grief and trauma you carry.

Far from being an avenue for fleeing our trials, meditation can assist us in facing what may feel uncomfortable and unsettling. But rather than simply dwelling on the source of difficulty, it is possible to allow ourselves to accept these awkward elements, eventually realizing that courageous reckoning with such feelings paves a path towards personal growth and healing.

By connecting with your own story, allowing your own experiences, and letting the surrounding beauty fill your soul, you can erase the fearful feelings attached to your painful experience of losing a loved one and cope with that traumatic experience. Give yourself the grace to embrace your hope for yesterday and tomorrow.

Instead of dwelling on less-than-ideal moments, why not focus our attention and energy on positive experiences? Take the time to savor those treasured memories, even if they are tiny sparks of joy. Let's open ourselves up to optimism and enjoy more deeply enriching moments!

Celebrate even the smallest bursts of enthusiasm and build lasting memories for yourself as you go! Instead of dwelling on past hurts, focus your energy on reflecting on fond recollections. Let them bring joy when they come up in thought.

Key Points

- If you focus on the positive, you'll see more light in your life. If you dwell on the negative, you'll see more shadows around you.

- Train your brain to admire the positivity already around you to cultivate positivity. Enrich optimism and deepen your positive experiences–even if they're small.

- Visualize yourself absorbing these moments of light and love.

- Let go of what no longer serves and uplift you to make more room for what does.

Exercise

Moon rituals are ancient practices that allow us to have sacred natural experiences. They inspire healing, intention, and self-love by tuning us into the moon and its many phases. For this chapter's practice, we will perform a moon ritual.
The moon's unique phrases remind us that change can be positive and magical.

Releasing and Letting Go:
Forest Bathing

01 Grab a pen and set off on an adventure to find a peaceful spot in nature -- preferably a place with trees, like a forest. Safely go in the evening time so that you can see the moon. Consider inviting a friend or loved one.

02 Find a tree that you feel drawn to and sit beneath it.

03 Write your intentions on the piece of paper. Maybe you intend to cultivate, enrich, and absorb the surrounding light.

04 Now, stand up and look up at the tree. Admire and absorb its beauty. Accept its beauty amidst any of its imperfections.

05 Look up at the moon. Soak in its beauty and let it nourish your acceptance of change, as it, too, goes through many phases.

06 Imagine yourself releasing and letting go of what's weighing on you --your grief, pain, and faulty memories. Imagine them floating to the sky and tucking behind the moon or leaves.

07 Now imagine your intentions glowing within you. Imagine them building and filling your heart and mind, giving you the capacity for positive change and acceptance.

08 When you're ready, take a deep breath.

Creating a Meditation Space for Healing

Objective: To understand the importance of meditating where you feel safe and how to create a meditation space for healing.

Your Environment Affects Your Energy

Even if we aren't aware of it, the people and surroundings around us constantly affect us. Think about how your energy and perception shift in a dark, loud restaurant versus a light, open space outside.

The sounds, sights, and senses attached to our environments stimulate our emotions. This is especially true for empaths, compassionate people, and those who've experienced trauma, grief, and loss.

Notice how your energy shifts in response to different people and places. With increased awareness, you can nurture yourself by surrounding yourself with the things that uplift you!

Meditate Where You Feel Safe & Secure

Meditation is an empowering method to open oneself up and create a safe space to reflect, recover, and build meaningful connections. Before beginning your journey inward, intuitively tune into the environment around you—find a peaceful corner where all your focus can stay on relaxation!

In moments of quiet reflection, we often expose ourselves to the pains and emotions of our past. But meditation is about compassionate acceptance. We are embracing all that has come before without judgment so that it no longer has power over us.

When we create a safe space for this inner work, we can cultivate a more meaningful connection with ourselves through awareness and understanding.

Unplug from the stress of daily life and find your inner peace in a place that lets you EXPRESS, BE PRESENT to appreciate new perspectives, REJUVENATE with some much-needed rest for body and soul, AWAKEN creativity or intuition within yourself through mindful practices, and CONNECT meaningfully to others. Entering this tranquil environment allows one to enjoy an open mindset free from unwanted distractions.

Elements of a Healing Meditation Space

Once you find your space, it's time to make it sacred to you.
Here are some elements of healing environments that might speak to your senses and make your space one of healing and purpose:

SIGHTS

Enhance your meditation space with candles, tea lights, or salt lamps. Hang paintings, photos, crystals, and other sights that elevate, comfort, and offer you hope if you think it's appropriate for your environment.

SOUNDS

Playing comforting binaural beats creates calm. Solfeggio frequencies are better for relaxing your nerves and settling you into a peaceful slumber. Solfeggio frequencies are nine different frequencies that all have specific health benefits. Become acquainted with frequencies that can promote relaxation, and positivity, and decrease anxiety.

BE PRESENT

Our sense of smell is deeply tied to our emotions. Studies show that our olfactory system has the most robust connection to our memories. Therefore, smelling an old family recipe or walking into your favorite park from childhood can transport you back in time.

Be intentional about the scent of your space with essential oils, candles, or incense.

TOUCH

Placing our hand on our heart while meditating can create a comforting sensation, fostering a deeper connection and cultivating a sense of grounding and presence.

THIS FIRST REQUIRES US TO GET COMFORTABLE.

While meditating, you can lie on a soft cushion or surface. Assemble blankets, pillows, or other comfort items, tuning into your senses for an authentic experience. This is your own personal sanctuary.

Key Points

- Our emotions are stimulated by the feelings associated with our surroundings. This is especially true for those who've experienced trauma, grief, and loss.

- The best meditation spot is neutral, allowing us to EMBRACE our desire to EXPRESS, BE PRESENT, REJUVENATE, AWARENESS, or CONNECT.

- Create a safe and pleasant environment by purposefully nurturing sights, sounds, fragrances, and touch sensations that feel appropriate for you.

Exercise

Let's set up a safe meditation space unique to YOU. Answer the questions and follow the prompts below to get started.

Grab your pen. We're going to express your feelings for your meditation space.

What sights and visuals uplift you?
Is it the mountains? A picture of loved ones? Lights, crystals, or lamps?

_____
_____
_____
_____
_____
_____
_____
_____

Once you determine those, gather them to form your space.

Now, what sounds uplift you?
Create a meditation playlist of songs or sounds that relax you and bring you comfort.

_____
_____
_____
_____
_____
_____
_____
_____

Next, what scents speak to you?
Whether incense, essential oils, or candles, gather scents that relax and rejuvenate your spirit.

_____
_____
_____
_____
_____
_____
_____
_____

Last, gather comfort items like blankets, pillows, etc., to comfort you by touch.

Once you've created your space, honor it and set it apart
as your sacred meditation space.

a. Get into a comfortable position.

b. Close your eyes. .

c. Take ten deep breaths, in and out.

Healing in Action:
Meditation Exercise for Trauma

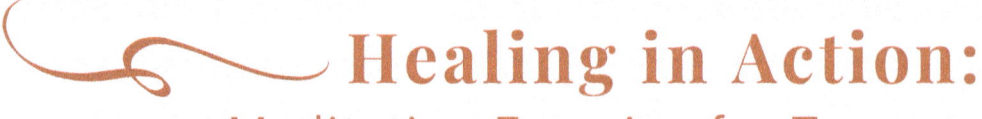

Objective: To identify the physical and emotional side effects of carrying unresolved trauma and how meditation can help us work through them

Releasing Unresolved Trauma

Trauma can be an invisible burden, lurking beneath the surface and weighing us down. Unresolved trauma often gets trapped in our bodies–suppressing emotions and resulting in physical symptoms that reflect inner turmoil. Healing from this suffering requires understanding how it lingers within us so that we may regain control over ourselves.

Although we often prioritize physical healing, the truth is that emotional wounds can be equally impactful on our overall health and happiness. Caring for our mental well-being should never take a back seat when cultivating inner peace.

To achieve true healing, we must first open ourselves up to awareness - taking the time to acknowledge our physical, mental, and emotional states. This enlightened voyage of self-discovery is required for everyone to undergo a healing metamorphosis.

Physical Wounds of Unresolved Trauma	Emotional Wounds of Unresolved Trauma
<ul><li>Physical stiffness and rigidity</li><li>Poor digestion</li><li>Insomnia</li><li>Restlessness</li></ul>	<ul><li>Poor emotional health</li><li>Slow responses</li><li>High sensitivity</li><li>Hyperarousal</li><li>Imbalance in attitude and behavior toward everything</li><li>Lack of concentration</li><li>Low self-esteem Disassociation</li></ul>

Meditation to Move with the Trauma of Losing Your Love One

Unresolved trauma can become an invisible sickness, damaging our mental and physical health until we feel completely immobilized. But there is still hope. Rather than pretending it never happened or burying it, working through the pain will result in profound healing.

We can reprogram our minds through contemplative practice to manifest contentment and joy. Meditation provides a powerful toolkit for facing life's challenges with resilient positivity rather than remaining restricted by past traumas or negativity. It allows us to confront difficult experiences openly yet compassionately— equipping us with the resources to survive and thrive!

Meditation can provide a pathway to healing from trauma, but the journey has challenges. Along with moments of connection and inner peace come vulnerability, discomfort, and sometimes painful memories that must be faced head-on before actual progress can be made.

Healing trauma can intimidate, but don't let it scare you away ––we're here to heal. So take a deep breath and have faith in yourself as you rediscover experiences that may have been forgotten or buried deep inside you. Let's journey to restore balance and find peace within ourselves.

Extend yourself the grace you so willingly give others.

Key Points

- Unresolved trauma gets stuck into your physical body, restricting and blocking your emotions.

- We profoundly affect our mental peace and physical well-being by tending to our emotional wounds.

- Meditation helps you rewire your brain for joy and happiness and endure traumatic experiences.

- It's not painless --but there's no need to be scared. It's all about grace, healing, and self-love.

 # Exercise

For this chapter's exercise, we're going to practice mindfulness. Mindfulness is a gentle, accessible way to gain the benefits of meditation, especially for those of us carrying unresolved trauma. Together, follow the prompts below:

01

Get into your safe meditation space and make yourself comfortable.

02

Once you're ready, close your eyes and draw attention to your breath.

03

Notice the natural flow of your regular breath. Notice the breath flow into your nose, fill your lungs, and rush back out. Extend thanks to your body for how naturally and effortlessly it does this for you.

04

After a few natural breaths, take one deep breath through your nose, counting from 1, 2, 3, 4, and 5.

05

Once you've fully inhaled, hold your breath for 1, 2, 3, 4, and 5. Notice how your lungs feel fully expanded.

06

Now exhale through your nose, 1, 2, 3, 4, 5.

07

Repeat this process 5-10 more times, paying attention to the sensations in your body. Pay attention to the movement and expansion of your lungs. Notice the cool air traveling down your throat on the inhale and the warm hair leaving your body on the exhale.

08

If you get distracted, don't worry. Gently shift your focus back to your bodily sensations. Get in tune with how you're feeling at this very moment.

09

After 5-10 deep breaths, practice this 5-10 more times, but this time, I want you to...

a. Imagine your body filling with light and healing on every inhale.

b. And on every hold, I want you to imagine the oxygen traveling through your veins, drawing out all the tension, resistance, and pain you've held onto.

c. On the exhale, I want you to imagine this tension and pain traveling up and leaving your body, disappearing as soon as it releases.

d. As you continue inhaling and exhaling, more and more light replaces this pain, and soon enough, your body and mind are glowing with light.

10

Once you've finished your practice, allow yourself to shift back to your natural breath and breathe in and out five times. When you're ready, open your eyes.

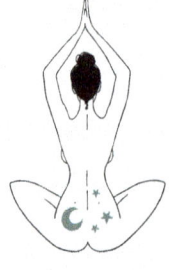

Meditation Techniques to Transition Purposefully Using the Body Scan Method

Objective: To understand the power of connecting with your body and honoring your needs of body scanning.

Checking in with YOU

Life is busy! And if you're a Heyoka Empath like me, you might take on others' emotions and needs as you move about your day. While caring for others is a beautiful, transformative gift, we must not forget to care for ourselves.

Self-care isn't selfish. Remember: You can't pour from an empty cup. It's time to fill it together (and even let it overflow!).

Checking in with yourself can be as simple as asking how you're doing daily. It can enlighten you with the ability to tune into and connect your body, mind, and spirit. As we go through the busyness of our days, it's almost easy to feel separated from our bodies, running on autopilot and going through the motions. This is incredibly tempting for those with heavy grief and loss.

Many trauma survivors feel alienated and dissociated from their bodies as if they observe and watch their life happen to them.

However, checking in with ourselves, connecting with our bodies, and expressing our feelings allows us to move through them. It fortifies us to build a lovely garden with our grieving tears and thrives our purpose out of agony. Meditation is all about becoming comfortable with the uncomfortable to EMBRACE and EMPOWER ourselves.

Check-in with you. Please be aware of your needs and honor them.

You are always deserving of this necessary yet transformational act of self-love.

The Body Scan Method

Body scanning is a mindfulness meditation practice focusing awareness on various body areas systematically and nonjudgmentally. Body scanning is intended to promote a deep sense of bodily awareness, which can aid in the release of tension and stress, increase relaxation, and develop a stronger connection with the present moment. Typically, a body scan begins with the feet and progresses gently through the legs, chest, arms, and head, paying attention to each body region.

As we bring attention to each area, one may notice sensations such as warmth, tingling, or tightness, and the goal is to observe these sensations without trying to change them. Body scanning can be useful for reducing anxiety, improving sleep, and boosting general well-being with frequent practice.

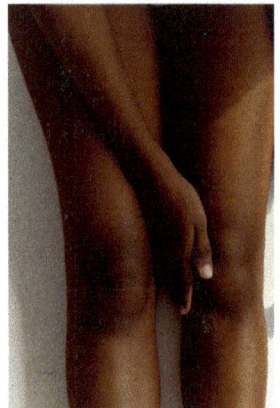 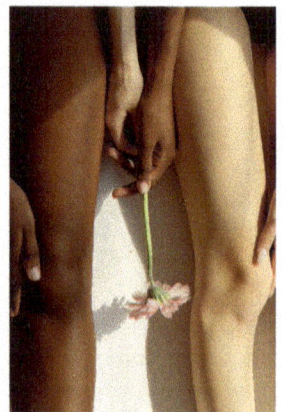 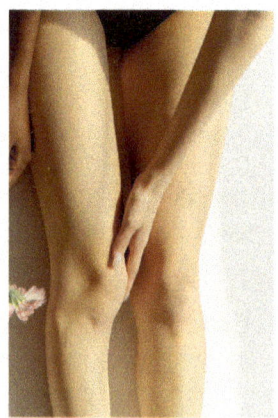

Body scanning seeks to reconnect and harmonize the mind and body. To speak with and be empowered by our bodies. Body scanning can bring you into the present moment. It might disclose what you require and how you should care for yourself now. It enables us to transition from autopilot to waking up to the beauty of the present moment.

Ultimately, the choice between body scanning and other types of meditation depends on preference and individual needs. Both methods can effectively promote mindfulness and enhance overall well-being, and individuals may benefit from incorporating both practices into their self-care routine.

All you need is 5 minutes each day. Let go of the chains of the past and future, let go of your to-do list, and let go of your need to make sure everyone else's cup is full for just a moment and take care of yourself—Check in with yourself.

Key Points

- Self-care isn't selfish.

- It's easy to feel separated from our bodies, running on autopilot and going through the motions.

- Checking in with ourselves, connecting with our bodies, and expressing these emotions empower us to move through them.

- Body scanning is mindfulness meditation that brings awareness to each body part.

- Bring your awareness to the here and now and shift your focus to what you need and how you can care for yourself today.

 # Exercise

QUIZ

What does self-care mean to you?

_____
_____
_____
_____

How can body scanning help us take care of ourselves through our grief?

_____
_____
_____
_____
_____

JOURNAL PROMPTS

How is your body feeling today?

_____
_____
_____
_____
_____
_____
_____
_____

What might that tension be from, physically?

_____
_____
_____
_____

What might that tension be from, emotionally?

_____
_____
_____
_____

What part(s) of your body feel strong, relaxed, or powerful?

_____
_____
_____
_____

What might you be doing to help them feel that way?

_____
_____
_____
_____

Action Prompt

> We're going to practice body scanning together. Find your safe meditation space, get comfortable, lie or sit down, and follow the prompts below.

01 Find a comfortable and quiet place to lie down on your back with your arms at your sides and your legs slightly apart. You can also sit in a chair if lying down is uncomfortable.

02 Close your eyes and take a few deep breaths, allowing your body to relax and your mind to become more focused.

03 Bring attention to your feet, noticing warmth, tingling, or tension. Spend a few moments focusing on your feet before moving to the next part of your body.

04 Slowly move your attention up through your legs, paying attention to any sensations in your calves, knees, thighs, and hips.

05 Continue to move your attention up through your torso, paying attention to your lower back, abdomen, chest, and upper back.

06 Move your attention to your arms, starting with your hands and moving up through your forearms, upper arms, and shoulders.

07 Finally, bring your attention to your head and neck, noticing any sensations in your face, jaw, neck, and scalp.

08 As you move through each part of your body, try to observe any sensations without judgment or analysis. Notice them and let them be.

09 Once you have completed the body scan, take a few moments to rest and be with any sensations that arise in your body.

10 When you're ready, slowly open your eyes and bring your attention back to the present moment.

You can practice this exercise for as long as you like, starting with a few minutes and gradually increasing the time as you become more comfortable with the practice.

Rituals for Remembrance:
Rite of Passage Moon Meditation

Objective: To explore the meaning of rituals and how you can create meditative rituals to remember, honor, and connect with your loved ones.

The Power of Rituals

Our journey has been filled with knowledge and inspiration, so let's take it further. Hold my hand as we harness your newfound wisdom to heal, strengthen relationships, and set daily goals through transformative rituals. Let's ignite your path to growth and fulfillment.

Repetition is powerful. Routine has the power to transform. When we cultivate attentive habits and uphold our healing rituals, we demonstrate to ourselves and the Universe that we are open to receiving—that we are willing to do whatever it takes to give our pain a purpose and tend to our gardens of grief.

Through rituals, we can remember and honor those who have passed away while also planting a loving seed of recollection in our souls. Incorporating these techniques into our daily lives fosters compassion in ourselves, allowing us to better recall and heal from loss.

It's all about intention with EMBRACE. It's about claiming the life we know we deserve—the life we know we're capable of—right now.

To help you create rituals of celebration and remembrance, I will energetically guide you so that you can connect with your loved ones, your past selves, and your energetic, endless future.

 Moon Rituals

Like the moon, we go through phases and times of brightness and darkness in our lives. The beauty is that no matter what misfortune comes our way or how difficult things appear, something will always stand firm, as the stable moon does throughout its cycles, never changing.

This balance of constancy and change can ground us in our journeys through the next chapters of our life without the actual presence of our loved ones. While our pain and grief may ebb and flow, the constancy of hope for healing and the spiritual presence of our loved ones never change.

Moon rituals—meditations that tap into our mysterious celestial sanctuary's different phases and energies—can help you harness the power of lunar energy. Step away from your everyday routine and join Mother Moon on an exhilarating meditation adventure!

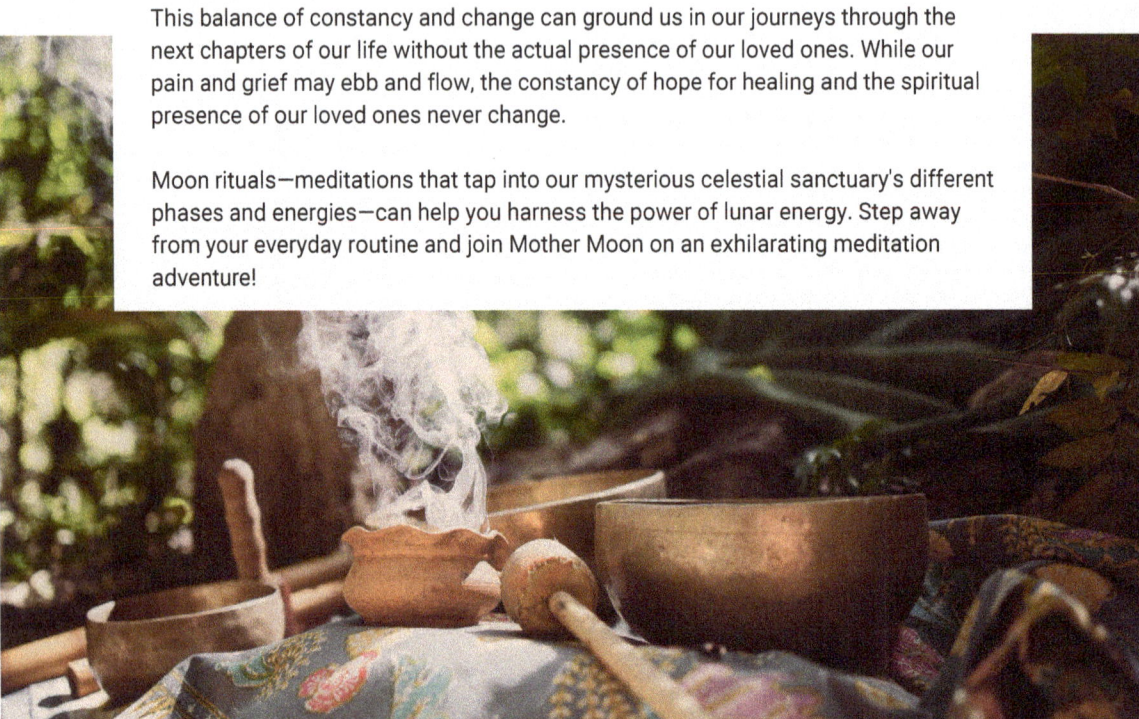

- When the moon waxes, you can create your ritual based on its manifestation and expansive energy. Manifest your future by journaling, meditating, and acting in abundance.

- When the moon wanes, you can honor your ritual and intention based on releasing, boundaries, and letting go. Could you let go of what no longer serves you? Write these words down, throw them away, take a warm bath, or even dance away the negative energy!

- When the moon is full, its energy is high, and you can find peace as you exhale and feel whole. Practice self-care and declutter your life of what might hold you back. You can even use the healing powers of rainwater to cleanse your energy.

Key Points

- When we create mindful habits and honor our healing routines, we show ourselves and the Universe that we're open to receiving.

- The moon is symbolic of our journey here on Earth. We go through phases, seasons, and moments of lightness, darkness, of feeling whole or incomplete.

- This balance of constancy and change can ground us in our journeys. While our pain and grief may ebb and flow, the endurance of hope for healing and the spiritual presence of our loved ones never changes.

- Waxing Moon Energy = Manifestation and abundance. Waning Moon Energy = Releasing.

- Full Moon = Cleansing and letting go.

Exercise

QUIZ

Why are rituals so powerful?

_____
_____
_____
_____

Why is the moon symbolic of our life journeys?

_____
_____
_____
_____

JOURNAL PROMPTS

How can you make meditation a ritual of remembrance and celebration of your loved one's life?

_____
_____
_____
_____
_____
_____
_____

What would you like to manifest and invite into your life during the Waxing Moon Energy?

_____
_____
_____
_____

What would you like to release and let go of in your life during the Waning Moon Energy?

_____
_____
_____
_____

What would you like to cleanse and care for in your life during the Full Moon?

_____
_____
_____
_____

Action Prompt

> Depending on the moon's phase, I want you to create a moon ritual centered on the love, compassion, and connection you feel toward your loved one who's transitioned. Focus on creating an altar in your heart, mind, and spirit of hope, healing, and remembrance. This positive energy around their memory can heal your heart and connect you with their spirit.
> It's time for EMBRACE.

Thank You for Choosing You.

You take a powerful step toward self-discovery by starting your recovery and creating your own self-modalities during prayer or meditation.

May the force of optimism guide you, may a purpose that both enlightens and inspires fuel your days and may you experience unparalleled growth on this path that was never our choosing.

You are, without a doubt, deserving of all life has to offer.

The Grief Warrior

Be Present
The Third Stage of Grief

EMBRACE

MICHELE C. BELL
THE GRIEF WARRIOR®

What does the word EMBRACE mean to you?

To me, embracing empowers.

Embracing is a step beyond acceptance.
We must first accept our grief to healing and embrace it.
Our grief is where authentic alignment happens.

It's where we find the purpose for our pain, growth in our grief, and love after loss.

It's where everything clicks, and it all makes sense.

That's why 7 Stages of Grief is all about EMBRACE.
I can't wait for you to begin to Pivot with Purpose in the next stage.
BE PRESENT!

Make that leap of faith.

You Got This!

you've made it

You are now ready to **EMBRACE** our Third Stage:

— be present —

That's the blessing and power of **pivoting with purpose.**

What are the 7 Stages of Grief Alignment?
Express. **M**editate.
Be Present. **R**ejuvenate.
Awaken. **C**onnect. **E**at Healthy.

Healing begins with acceptance and alignment transforms us through embracing our life's experiences.

The empower of embracing is in your next chapter – are you ready to turn the page?

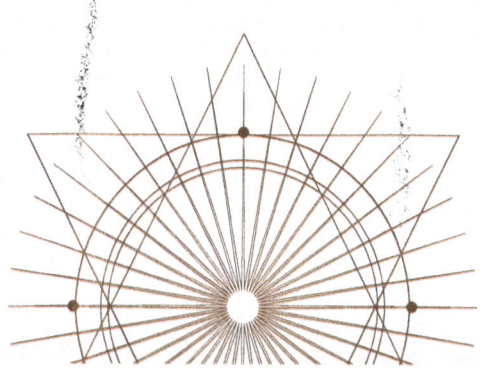

Table of Contents

Finding Presence in Grief	01
Healing Your Connection	04
Being Present In Pain	07
Embrace to Empower	10
Liberate Your Heart	13
Acceptance to Embrace	17
One Moment at a Time	20
Moment-ous Occasions	23
Sensitivity is Your Superpower	26
Strength in Sensitivity	29

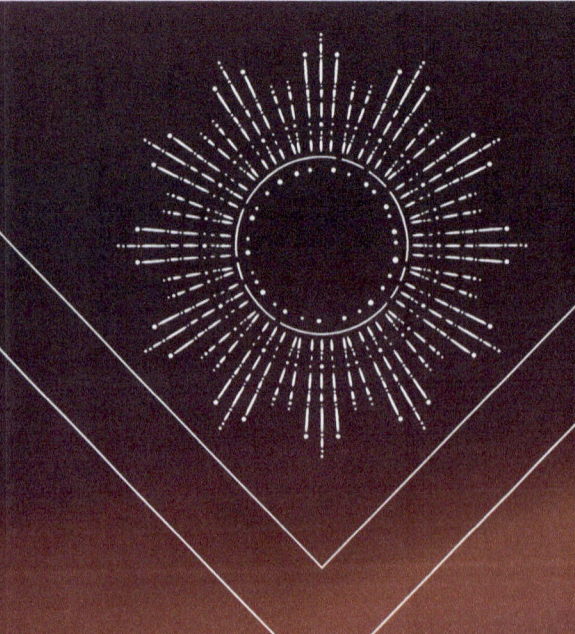

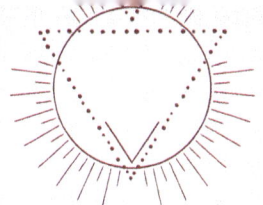

Finding Presence *with* Grief

A note of love

Transforming Grief into Growth: Navigating the Journey with Resilience and Purpose

Grief is an inevitable part of life's journey, and while experiencing pain may be unavoidable, it doesn't have to be without purpose. Everyone's experience is unique, and it can be challenging to remember this when all we have in common is suffering.

By engaging with our emotions and staying present in the moment, we can begin to make meaningful connections between pain and growth. This unlocks new levels of resilience and helps us find direction and renewed love for life.

Incorporating Solitude for Self-Reflection

The journey through grief can be long and arduous, but it is possible to emerge on the other side feeling healed. One often overlooked component of this journey is solitude. Taking time alone can provide valuable insight into our emotions, helping us navigate difficult waters toward peace and self-connection.

Embracing the Power of Being Human

Finding our inner strength during grief requires us to embrace the power of being human. It is essential to allow ourselves a safe place to cry and process our emotions honestly and authentically rather than masking them with false joy.

Balancing Solitude and Support

While being with loved ones during isolation can bring comfort, solitude can allow us to process our emotions without fear or judgment. To heal from grief effectively, we must listen intently to ourselves, finding the perfect balance between our need for solitude and the comforting embrace of others. Seeking support when necessary is also crucial for a balanced recovery.

By embracing our emotions, allowing ourselves room for self-expression, and finding balance in solitude and support, we can transform grief into growth, emerging from the journey with newfound resilience and purpose.

Journal Prompts

Take some time to think about how grief can play a role in your journey. Is there a way to find meaning and personal growth through the experience of pain and loss?

_____
_____
_____
_____
_____
_____
_____
_____

Explore the balance between embracing your emotions and connecting to the present moment. How can you build a connection between your grief and personal resilience, allowing for new directions and love in your life?

_____
_____
_____
_____
_____
_____
_____
_____

Consider the role of solitude in your grief journey. How can taking time alone provide insight while seeking support and connection from trusted loved ones? How can you balance solitude and social support for a balanced recovery?

_____
_____
_____
_____
_____
_____
_____
_____

Exercise

For every chapter exercise, locate a peaceful area and focus on being fully present.

Coping with grief can be a challenging process. However, by practicing mindfulness and creating a peaceful environment for yourself, you can find inner calmness and guide yourself through this difficult journey.

- Imagine you've stepped outside of yourself and your experience.

- Take an inward journey and be your best friend, understanding you with love and compassion.

- As this observer, you've just been told it's your responsibility to understand, support, and extend empathy to this person.

- How do you view your grief experience from this higher, outside perspective?

- As this compassionate observer, how do you respond to these experiences? What words of love and wisdom do you share?

Why not speak kind words to yourself? Take a moment to jot them down as though you're penning a letter to your future self in your diary.

It's important to take time each day to relax and find inner peace. Even just a few minutes can make a difference. Focusing on your breath can help you stay present and calm, leading to a better understanding and resolution of your emotions. Consider incorporating mindfulness into your healing routine.

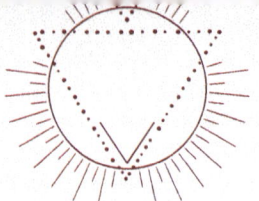

healing your connection

Even though we feel the pain of our losses, grief helps us acknowledge that there was once something unique and valuable in our lives.

A connection still exists with those who have passed on—a supernatural force for healing, hope, and courage to carry forward their legacy.

In my son's situation, his guiding light is ever-present, transcending death by providing opportunities to appreciate beauty and blessings from above.

He led me here to you.

Our connection with our departed loved ones transcends the physical world. Experiences and testimonies from many reveal that death is only a doorway to an existence where we can remain in constant communion. While it may look and feel different, this connection with our loved ones is everlasting, even beyond the veil, if we are open to receiving the messages between the PAUSE.

To tune into this connection, we must find presence. The PAUSE allows us to slow down and accept what is ahead without expectation or judgment; it's time to embrace stillness.

It might lead you to your next great story.

The Release Mantra

"I release all that no longer has a purpose within me. I call in my center of pause and knowing. I ask it to embellish my being with wisdom and dissolve away heavy burdens by releasing and letting go. I ask my inner spirit to trust the process. I understand deeply what you have taught me. I honor every experience with love in my being. The pieces of me are restored." Blessed Be

Journal Prompts

Express the unique and valuable aspects of your life that your losses have made you more aware of. How has grief helped you acknowledge the significance of what was once present?

_____
_____
_____
_____
_____
_____
_____
_____

Explore the supernatural force of healing, hope, and courage that comes from maintaining a connection with your departed loved ones. How has this connection provided opportunities to appreciate beauty and blessings?

_____
_____
_____
_____
_____
_____
_____
_____

Share a personal experience or testimony that highlights how your loved one's guiding light continues to influence and lead you. How has their presence transcended death and inspired you to embrace new opportunities and paths?

_____
_____
_____
_____
_____
_____
_____

Exercise

When completing each chapter exercise, it's important to locate a peaceful environment and practice mindfulness.

Finding a quiet space and practicing mindfulness can be helpful in the grieving process.

- Find your way to Pause today. Listen to your inner sanctuary.

- Picture yourself as a ball of white energy. Releasing and Letting Go.

- Maybe it's simply sitting without looking at your phone, watching TV, or responding to the noise. Take a pause, even if it's just for 5 minutes.

- When you are STILL listening to the telepathic waves, write down the messages.

- If you need to, be still in nature. Be still while listening to calming music. However you 'be still' today, know that you are making peace with the present moment and showing yourself and your higher power that you are one step closer to embracing.

Consider the power of finding presence and embracing stillness to tune into the connection with your departed loved ones.

How can you create moments of pause to be open to receiving their messages and guidance?

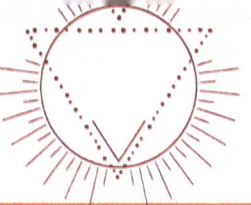

being present in pain

We recognize that simply being present for others can be a powerful way of expressing our support.

I am only here with you right now because of my losses.

What once felt like stumbling blocks became my stepping stones, lifting me to guide and serve others and navigate life after loss.

But even now, I am reminded that forward progress can only come when we embrace our wounds; this allows us to persevere in love.

In finding presence in our pain, we can also find purpose.

Faced with heartbreaking loss, grieving can be an unexpected source of strength and resilience. When we open ourselves to compassion and service—offering kindness and expecting nothing in return—we can connect more deeply with life. This powerful choice allows us to move forward courageously, despite our sorrows.

Let's all take inspiration from those who have overcome adversity. By learning from our struggles, we can discover a greater sense of purpose that will bring peace to ourselves and others on this journey ahead. May we each find blessings along the way!

We can turn our losses into opportunities for growth and connection with others. To begin, we should focus on being kind and supportive of ourselves in the present moment.

Journal Prompts

Reflect on how your losses have shaped your journey and led you to where you are today. How have your stumbling blocks become stepping stones, guiding you to serve others and navigate life after loss?

_____
_____
_____
_____

Explore the significance of embracing your wounds and persevering in love. How has finding presence in your pain allowed you to find purpose and move forward with courage and resilience?

_____
_____
_____
_____

Share a story of when your grief became a source of strength and resilience. How did opening yourself to compassion and service, offering kindness without expecting anything in return, deepen your connection with life?

_____
_____
_____
_____

Consider the transformational power of turning losses into opportunities for growth and connection. How can you practice self-kindness and support in the present moment, allowing yourself to embrace the blessings and possibilities ahead?

_____
_____
_____
_____

Exercise

For each chapter exercise, make it a point to find a peaceful setting and stay focused on the present moment.

Finding a quiet space and practicing mindfulness can be helpful in the grieving process.

Create a Voice Memo on your phone with the exercise below.

- Find a quiet, meditative space to relax in.

- Once you've found a comfortable position, sit or lie down. Close your eyes between reading each exercise step.

- Now, visualize your pain as a light in your body. This light could be in your head, heart, belly, or body.

- When this light becomes trapped within you, it causes discomfort. That's OK. Allow it to be there by sitting with it.

- Now, imagine what happens when you share this light with others ––it becomes much less heavy and painful. It helps others more than you could've ever imagined.

- All these months or years of carrying this light within you feel less painful because you created purpose. You helped others share their light and feel guided by yours.

- When you're ready, open your eyes and write down your thoughts.

Prioritizing Self-Care: Mindful Journaling Exercises for Inner Peace

Did you know that speaking kind and encouraging words to yourself can be incredibly helpful? Take a moment to write them down in your journal as if you're penning a letter to yourself. Incorporating mindfulness into your life demands that you pause and reflect. Try these journal prompts and exercises to help you live in the present and ultimately find inner peace amidst the chaos of everyday life.

embrace to empower

It's our instinct to run away from pain.

It's a habit to avoid what makes us uncomfortable at all costs.

But we can never move forward if we constantly run away from pain! It will only make the pain more painful and the discomfort more challenging.

So, we'll still feel some resistance when we go against our learned nature and approach our pain, loss, and grief with extended arms. We might even feel a bit threatened.

Embracing uncertainty makes us realize our true strength; pushing ourselves out of our comfort zone can be frightening but ultimately leads to greater confidence.

And then we're finally able to rest. We don't have to run, hide, or fear anymore.

We can sit with the pain, empower our inspiration, and grow and develop resilience on the grief journey. The only way is through diligent commitment leading to discernment.

Release the weight of yesterday, as this moment holds boundless potential and promise. When we fully engage with today, we can use it to mend old wounds and gain strength from our aspirations. Even amidst uncertainty, we can find safety by embracing the present moment.

Discover inner peace and happiness by embarking on a journey of self-reflection. Mindfulness, self-awareness, and resilience are essential for achieving a fulfilling life.

Journal Prompts

You were designed to be different on purpose.

Reflect on a time when you instinctively ran away from pain or discomfort. How did this avoidance affect your ability to move forward and find a resolution?

___

When approaching your pain, loss, and grief head-on, explore the resistance and fear. How can you shift your mindset to see these moments as opportunities for growth and inner strength?

___

Consider the power of embracing uncertainty and stepping out of your comfort zone. How can you cultivate confidence and resilience by confronting challenging situations and exploring new possibilities?

___

What transformative lessons have you learned by sitting with your pain and embracing discomfort on your journey of healing and growth?

___

Exercise

Locating a peaceful area and focusing on being fully present is essential.

Mornings are best - our theta brain is most active in receiving messages.

- Get 1% more comfortable with the uncomfortable today—nothing major, just a tiny way to show strength.

- Maybe you call up a trusted friend and talk about your feelings. Perhaps you journal, create art, and meditate internally on your creative work.

- Create a map destination you would like to travel to in honor of your grief journey.

- Maybe you decide to go on a 1:1 healing retreat. Choose the destination. Check in with me about your location before you commit!

- Routines with intention are important. Dedicate 15 days a month to Eating Healthy. Book a consultation with me to set this up!

Spend time writing in your journal and listing words that strengthen you. Reflect on your blessings and write an encouraging letter telling yourself that it's okay to take a breather and appreciate your accomplishments.

You Got This, Warrior

liberate your heart

What Does Acceptance Mean?

These widely known 5 stages of grief may only *partially* capture the complex and individual nature of our healing journeys.

Denial.
Anger.
Bargaining.
Depression.
And finally, acceptance.

When it comes to coping with loss, we all have our own distinct stories. Sorrow is a profoundly personal experience, and the traditional stages of sorrow may not always reflect this. Viewing your emotional path as a winding road rather than a rigorous series of steps may be more helpful. Remember that you are not required to follow any one path; everyone's sorrow is unique and will guide them toward healing.

Grief is a complicated and intensely personal experience with the potential for five distinct emotions. But these shouldn't limit our journey. - Instead, we should consider an ongoing exploration of grief that doesn't narrow down any emotion as negative or underdeveloped. Here lies the opportunity to embrace each moment without judgment or stigma attached.

Grief can be a powerful adversary, but you are encouraged to welcome it here. Although carrying grief takes strength, shying away from its presence will only delay proper recovery. Give your pain permission to enter and linger awhile so that it may slowly move through you until there is space for healing within the hollows of your heart.

Acknowledge what is hard for you and embrace this moment as a chance for transformation.

It's important to take a break and enjoy the present moment. Don't worry about what you "should" be doing; pay attention to your body's needs. Take the time to care for yourself without criticism and acknowledge how your body feels.

It's Time to Prioritize Your Emotional Well-being

Take a moment to focus on your emotions and give yourself the time and space you need to experience them. Don't suppress your feelings; permit yourself to feel compassionate – every emotion counts!

Embrace honesty and bravery; don't hesitate to express your emotions. Your story is unique and valuable; don't shy away from sharing it with the world. Take a leap of faith, courageously open up about your feelings, and experience the strength of connecting with the present moment.

Journal Prompts

Reflect on a recent small win or accomplishment that brought you joy or a sense of fulfillment. Describe how it made you feel and how it impacted your overall well-being.

_____
_____
_____
_____
_____
_____
_____
_____

Explore moments in your life when you demonstrated self-love and self-respect. What choices or actions did you take to prioritize your mental, physical, or spiritual well-being? How did these choices positively impact your life?

_____
_____
_____
_____
_____
_____
_____
_____

How can you incorporate small acts of self-care and self-love into your daily routine? How can you prioritize and make space for these activities to cultivate a deeper sense of self-compassion and inner liberation?

_____
_____
_____
_____
_____
_____
_____

Exercise

Find a quiet space - Be Present.

Doing things with INTENTION will build awareness in your PAUSE journey.

- Lean into your emotions and live in the now. Care for them.

- Healthily accept your sadness. Perhaps it's writing in a journal, ranting to a trusted friend, listening to melancholy music, or simply crying.

- Lean into your feelings of optimism.

- Allow yourself to be furious if you are feeling angry.

- It's not about letting your emotions drive or control you --it's about giving them space to come and go in your body so they don't prevent you. Accept to embrace. Embrace release.

Empower Yourself with Self-Affirmations
Incorporate positive self-talk into your daily routine by writing affirmations in your journal. Pen a letter to yourself that expresses the words you need to hear.
Feel the sense of liberation coursing through your heart as you take each step towards breaking free from the chains that once held you back. Celebrate small victories along the way and honor yourself with unwavering self-love and respect. This is your journey to liberation, where you rise and soar with the boundless freedom that resides within you.

acceptance to embrace

Loving deeply comes at the expense of grief, a heavy load to bear when our loved ones depart from us. I have experienced this - a sense of hollowness that can seem overwhelming during times of sadness.

We do not seek to bury our loved ones' memories with a fast and superficial solution. Instead, this is an opportunity for us to commemorate their absence in a meaningful way that genuinely pays tribute to them and revels in life.

Through its inclusion, authentic acceptance allows us to explore the depths of our common space, modifying and expanding it as we rediscover life.

Grief and purpose can coexist in harmony - a beautiful journey of self-discovery. It's finding your WHY. It's letting our loving guardian angels guide us to a higher purpose. ––just like my son Nicky led me here to you.

Moving beyond grief can be liberating. Embracing loss can open the door to healing and a deeper appreciation of life's joys.

While life will never be the same again, a new route exists. Allow your sorrows, joys, frustrations, and expectations to accompany the ride - it's okay! This journey promises something fresh but allows you to honor what has been lost or changed forever.

Accepting and embracing this moment is the first step toward healing. Accept to embrace. Embrace to liberate.

Journal Prompts

Embrace Your Why

Reflect on a moment when you experienced the weight of grief and hollowness due to the departure of a loved one. How did this sadness impact you, and how did you navigate it?

_____
_____
_____
_____

Explore ways to commemorate the absence of your loved ones in a meaningful and authentic way. How can you create tributes and rituals that honor their memory and bring a sense of celebration to their life?

_____
_____
_____
_____

Consider the coexistence of grief and purpose in your journey. How can you find your "why" and allow the guidance of your loving guardian angels, like your loved one, to lead you toward a higher purpose? How can embracing loss and honoring what has been lost open the door to healing and a deeper appreciation of life's joys?

_____
_____
_____

What is your WHY?

_____
_____
_____
_____

Exercise

Locate a serene environment and remain attentive in the present moment.
Discernment is the root of Your Evolution.

- Find a comfortable position, whether sitting or lying down.

- Once you're ready, think about your life at this very moment. Not the past or future: the NOW. What is happening right now?
- Let the 'good' and 'bad' coexist.

- Now, take a deep breath through your nose and mouth. Think about what you have control over right now.

- Think about what you are willing to accept right now.

- Take three more deep breaths in and out, and think about how this present moment serves and empowers you.

Remind yourself of the words that will make you feel better. Write them down in your journal as if writing a letter to yourself.

Our health is fluid; simply getting by daily brings you closer to premature aging and disease. To have an abundance on your journey, you must WIN every day.

Small victories occur regularly. The decision to nourish your mind, body, and soul regularly shows SELF LOVE & SELF RESPECT.

Allow this to be your RISE meditation.

one moment at a time

The Alchemy of Presence and Gratitude on the Grief Journey

Time can feel like both an enemy and a savior in the labyrinth of grief. The past haunts, the future looms, and the present moment often gets lost in the shuffle. Yet, it's in the "now" that we find our most potent elixir for healing—presence.

Being present isn't about ignoring the pain or glossing over the complexity of emotions. It's about anchoring yourself in the current moment, allowing yourself to feel, breathe, and exist. When triggers arise, as they inevitably will, the practice of presence becomes your sanctuary.

Reflective Prompt:
What's one situation that recently triggered you? How did you react? Reimagine that moment, but anchor yourself in your presence this time. What changes?
Spinning thoughts into gratitude is the next layer of this alchemy. Gratitude in grief may sound paradoxical, but it's not about being thankful for the loss; it's about finding shards of light in the darkness. It's the warm hug from a friend, the comforting words that resonate, the newfound strength you never knew you had.

Reflective Prompt:
Think of a recent moment when you successfully combined presence and gratitude. How did it feel? What impact did it have on your journey?
Remember, the journey through grief is not a sprint but a marathon, and each moment of presence and gratitude is a step forward. Take it one moment at a time.

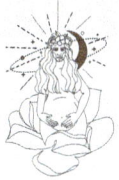

Journal Prompts

Embrace This Moment

Identify one moment of darkness on your grief journey. Can you find a shard of light within it? What are you grateful for in that moment?

_____
_____
_____
_____

Explore the power of mindfulness in releasing the burden of past regrets and future worries. How can you cultivate peace and healing by focusing on the present moment and letting go of what you cannot control?

_____
_____
_____
_____

Take advantage of the chance that every new day presents.
How can you approach today with intention and claim it as your own? How can you show up fully and make the most of this day?

_____
_____
_____
_____

Consider the idea od of surrendering to the present moment. What does it mean to let go of resistance and accept the circumstances as they are? How can embracing surrender bring peace and empowerment to your journey through grief?

_____
_____
_____
_____

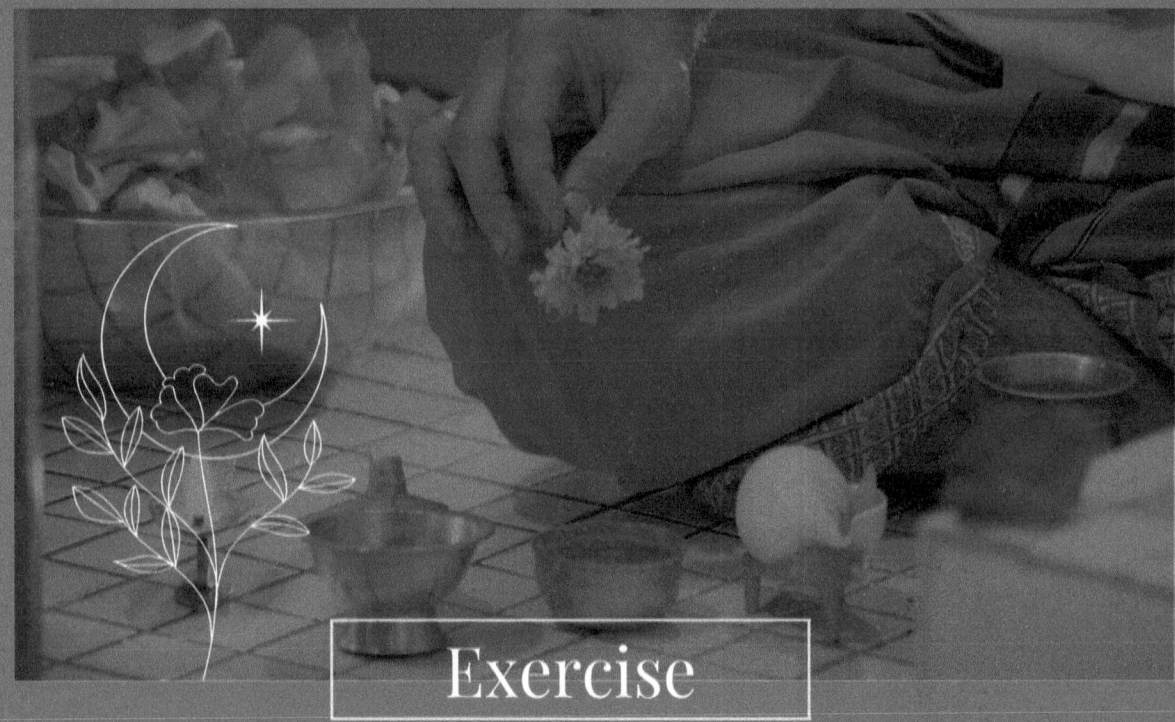

Exercise

Find a quiet space - Be Present.

Observance is the root of Your Elevation.

- Find a comfortable position to sit or lie down comfortably.

- Take five deep breaths through your nose and five deep breaths out through your mouth.

- Now, draw attention to your surroundings. Look for and name five things you can see in your environment in your head.

- Next, draw attention to and name four things you can feel around you. Maybe it's the ground at your feet, the warmth of your shirt, or the texture of the chair or table you're sitting at.

- Now, find two things you can smell. Our smell is one of the most potent emotional senses we have. Draw your awareness to be present with it.

- Lastly, find one thing you can taste. Whether it's mindfully taking a bite of chocolate or feeling the incredible sensation of water in your mouth, be present with your fifth sense.

Capture the beauty of life in your notebook; write it all down as notes or poems for posterity. These morsels of experience might inspire future creative pursuits and provide insight into a memorable period!

moment-ous occasions

Grand Rising Warrior. I want you to rediscover the joy of the present moment.

I know. It's challenging to do that when your mind is elsewhere, whether in the future or the past.

But we discover actual healing joy here at this moment.

Most "negative" emotions are associated with the past or the future; sadness, loss, and rage connect us to the past, but worry, tension, and fear drag us into the future.

These feelings are very normal. We can heal and go forward by embracing them, as you know.

But when these emotions become our 'default mode,' it's challenging to keep going. It becomes increasingly more difficult to find joy today.

So, we're here to embrace this moment and make it our own by using what I call "Moment-ous Occasions."

Moment-ous Occasions are intentional, present-based actions we can design to focus on the here and now.

It's taking a normal moment and turning it into something extraordinary. It accepts your emotions, recognizes your experiences, and embraces your pain.

It's leaning into the here and now and letting it be enough. It's putting on your "near-sighted glasses" and focusing on what is happening right before you.

Allow yourself to be satisfied if you are happy. Allow yourself to be sad if you are sad. There is no sense of shame or guilt here. There are no "shoulds" or "should'ves" in this sentence.

Embrace the feelings, surroundings, and experiences surrounding you today; make them yours.

Dare to share your emotions. Dare to say their name. Share your story.

Journal Prompts

The More You Share The More You Heal

What everyday moments can you turn into "Moment-ous Occasions" to fully embrace the present moment and find joy in the here and now?
_____
_____
_____

How can you cultivate a mindset of acceptance and non-judgment towards your emotions, experiences, and pain, allowing yourself to fully experience and embrace them without shame or guilt?
_____
_____
_____
_____

How can you create a safe and supportive space for yourself to share your emotions, story, and experiences? How can opening up and expressing your truth contribute to healing and growth on this journey?
_____
_____
_____
_____

Remember, the power to transform your journey lies within your hands. Embrace the present, honor your emotions, and create a life filled with purpose, joy, and limitless possibilities. The moment is yours to seize. What will you do with it?
_____
_____
_____
_____

Exercise

Find a quiet space - Be Present.

Rising is the Root of Your Healing.

- Choose how to make this moment memorable based on your responses.

- Stay calm. Do these exercises in moderation.

- Make a memory map of your trips with your loved one.

- Put a star next to you the memories that inspired your loved one.

- How can you make one of those experiences a momentous project honoring a special day or holiday coming up?

- Pick a date and invite friends and family to celebrate their life. Make it happen, whether it's a trip to that site or a virtual celebration.

You are not extending your grief journey by making these experiences come to life. These are healing-it-forward modalities for your soul. These expressions create comforting moments during the hard moments.

Embrace the power within you to honor your grief and find solace during life's most difficult moments.

sensitivity is your superpower

Vulnerability is Bravery.

Sometimes, it feels like vulnerability is a sign of weakness.

We suppress our tears and emotions and put on a "brave" face.

But when it comes down to it, running away from vulnerability is an act of fear. We discover courage in facing vulnerability—with its raw pain, beauty, and sorrow.

Embrace the present moment without reservation. Allow your emotions to arise and create a safe space for them to heal alongside you. Make yourself at home in their company.

Journal Prompts

Close your eyes. Listen to your Inner Warrior

What steps can you take to establish a secure and nurturing environment that allows your emotions to surface and be recognized?

___

What is embracing vulnerability like, and how can it contribute to your healing journey?

___

How can you cultivate a sense of comfort and acceptance in the presence of your emotions, allowing them to guide you toward healing and growth?

___

How can you actively embrace vulnerability, unlock your inner strength, and create a safe space for your emotions to heal and thrive?

___

Exercise

Find a quiet space - Be Present.
The Pause. Take a Moment. Sit with this.

- Sit or lie down and find a quiet place to meditate.

- Consider a genuine, vulnerable emotion that best reflects your sadness. Give this feeling a name, a color, a shape, or even a face.

- Now, invite this emotion in. Make space for it in your home and life.

- Imagine yourself introducing this emotion to your loved ones. Picture it making itself at home and following you in your everyday life.

- This emotion will fade as you become more at ease. You make the most of your time together. Any unfavorable characteristics you envisioned have faded. It makes sense to develop a strong, brave side of yourself.

> **What are the consequences of not being vulnerable?**
>
> no Growth
> no Strength
> no Confidence
> no Accountability
> no Discernment
> Always Be Mindful of Boundaries.

strength in sensitivity

The Power of Sensitivity: Embracing Your Authentic Self

Expressions like "stop being so emotional" or "don't be dramatic" are often used by people who are afraid of vulnerability. However, your sensitivity can be a source of strength, a superpower, and an authentic inner sanctuary.

It's easy to numb ourselves by getting lost in the busyness of everyday life or covering up our wounds with a band-aid. But it takes courage to face the toughest corners of our hearts. Being a strong yet vulnerable person is no small feat. It requires acknowledging our deepest emotions and deciding to heal instead of letting our wounds fester.

You possess a powerful combination of strength, sensitivity, and bravery. While letting go of the past may be challenging, choosing to heal will only make you stronger.

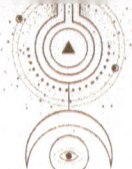

Journal Prompts

Our Strength is Found in the Uncomfortable Moments

Embrace your sensitivity as a source of strength. How can you harness your unique sensitivity to empower yourself and positively impact your life?
_____
_____
_____
_____

Break free from the chains of societal expectations. Challenge the notion that being emotional or dramatic is a weakness. How can you embrace and celebrate your authentic self, honoring the warrior with your emotions and experiences?
_____
_____
_____
_____

Dare to be vulnerable and dive deep into the depths of your heart. How can you summon the courage to confront and heal your inner wounds, knowing that true strength lies in embracing your vulnerabilities?
_____
_____
_____
_____

How can you actively release the past and fully embrace the healing process, allowing yourself to thrive in the present moment?
_____
_____
_____
_____

Exercise

**We are at another rebirth near ending the third stage. Take a Breath.
What a beautiful moment you've accomplished in your journey.**

- As we close our time together, I want you to take a deep breath and acknowledge where you are.

- Is it different from where you were when we first started together?

- Recognize your progress, no matter how small Embracewhere you are right now. It is enough

- Picture this very moment, strengthening your body from head to toe. Imagine this relief, presence, and 'enough-ness' washing over you. It fills you, bringing your strength, peace, and purpose.

- This moment is yours. Claim it. Tune in, heal, and OWN IT.

Unleash Your Inner Strength by Embracing Vulnerability
Don't be afraid to show your raw emotions and embrace your vulnerability. This authenticity can be empowering, and helps you to truly embark on a healing journey. Allow your emotions to guide you to a place of growth and resilience.

Thank You:
A Bow to Your Journey

Grand Rising Warrior,

Our time together has been brief, but we've already been through a lot. I sense your presence, your heart, and your optimism. Your healing journey has just begun.

I appreciate your presence and willingness to EMBRACE this moment. It's a moment meant for you, and I'm humbled to be a part of it in any way possible.

I encourage you to lean into this moment as there is great purpose, power, and presence. Remember that you deserve it all and that you are capable of achieving anything. You got this!

Stay strong and courageous,

Mama Warrior

REJUVENATE
The Forth Stage of Grief

EMBRACE

MICHELE C. BELL
THE GRIEF WARRIOR®

you've made it

You are now ready to **EMBRACE** our fourth Stage:

rejuvenate

That's the blessing and power of **pivoting with purpose.**

What are the 7 Stages of Grief Alignment?
Express. **M**editate.
Be Present. **R**ejuvenate.
Awaken. **C**onnect. **E**at Healthy.

Healing begins with acceptance and alignment transforms us through embracing our circumstances.

The empower of embracing is in your next chapter – are you ready to turn the page?

Table of Contents

Discovering What Rejuvenation Means To You 03
Creating A New Way To Navigate 08
Honoring Your Loved Ones 15
Honoring Your Emotions 22
Kicking Up Your Seratonin 28
Exploring New, High-Vibe Routes Of Rejuvenation 33

Discovering What Rejuvenation Means For You

OBJECTIVE:

To create your definition of rejuvenation, discover what makes you feel most excited about life, and let it rejuvenate your soul!

A Note of Love:
What Does it Mean to Rejuvenate?

No grief journey is the same. So why are we still treating them like they are?

No more following the outdated 5 Stages of Grief or cookie-cutter methods. Your story is yours, and it's your turn to write the next chapter.

This one's going to be fun! Together, we'll relax, recharge, and (you guessed it) rejuvenate. You might think, "But Michele, what does that mean?"

If you ask the dictionary, it'll tell you that to rejuvenate is:

"To make young or youthful again."

"Give new vigor to."

"To restore to an original or new state."

But since you're the author of this journey, it's up to you to write your definition of rejuvenation!

For me, it's the harmony of the old and new. Paying tribute to the past and embracing the present is what it is. It's like feeling alive and excited about life again! It's reconnecting, envisioning my best life, going on spontaneous trips, practicing self-care, tuning into my divinity, and simply finding restoration in every deep breath.

Rejuvenation may hit you like lightning. Or, a slow, steady sun might fuel your soul and start your next chapter—rise, gradually spreading light and energy on what's right before you. A reset button that wakes you up.

It's time to start living. It's time to unwind. It's time to rejuvenate.

Journal Prompts
What does rejuvenate mean to me?

Reflect on your unique grief journey: What aspects set your experience apart from others?

_____
_____
_____
_____

Define your version of rejuvenation. What does it mean to "feel most alive and excited about life"? Be the author of your rejuvenation story!

_____
_____
_____
_____

Harmonize the past and present: How can you pay tribute to your past while fully embracing the present?

_____
_____
_____
_____
_____

What small step can you take today to begin embracing the power of rejuvenation in your life?

_____
_____
_____
_____
_____

Journal Prompts
What does rejuvenate mean to me?

When I think of rejuvenation, what images or feelings come to mind?

Take a moment to visualize what it means to you personally.

_____
_____
_____
_____
_____
_____

Reflect on a time when you felt completely rejuvenated. What activities or experiences led to that feeling?

How can you incorporate more of those elements into your life?

_____
_____
_____
_____
_____
_____

Consider any obstacles or barriers preventing you from experiencing rejuvenation in your life.

How can you overcome these challenges and create space for rejuvenation to thrive?

_____
_____
_____
_____
_____
_____

Exercise

- Choose an environment, term, or action from your journal prompt responses. How could you make it a reality in your daily life?

- Consider yourself energized by activities that delight you, such as going to your favorite park, listening to motivating music, or engaging in self-care.

- Envision an intense beam of light flooding your being with a new sense of optimism and strength. Imagine the appearance and sensation of the light - it could be any hue you prefer. It may be warm, cool, or empowering.

- Allow this light to guide you in your quest for rejuvenation. Let it infuse your being like a tranquil sunrise or a powerful lightning bolt.

- Take some time to describe the energizing light that you are currently feeling. Try to be detailed and let your creative side flow freely. This description will help you to remember this feeling in the future, whether you do something rejuvenating or visualize the light filling your soul. Let yourself have some fun with it!

Creating a New Way to Navigate

OBJECTIVE:

To map out your current grief navigation and reroute it toward growth, healing, and purpose.

A Note of Love:
How Are You Currently Navigating Your Grief?

Why not take a different route and allow the fresh air to rejuvenate your spirit? Breaking out of your routine is crucial for your well-being.

The grieving process is not just a momentary interruption or a solitary occurrence.

It is an entirely new course and direction in our existence, and we need a different way of navigating this unfamiliar territory.

Assessing your current place on the journey is critical to navigating your grief process effectively.

How are you coping with your loss? Is it actively influencing you, or is it directing you? Or do you let it rule you? Let's have an open discussion about it.

I assure you there are no right or wrong answers, only the need for honesty and self-awareness.

Allow time and space to process sadness. Reflecting on emotions can improve understanding and emotion management.

It's easy to run out of fuel on this journey, to become fatigued, exhausted, and feel like giving up on trying to move forward for weeks, months, or even years.

But I'm here to remind you to fill your tank. Fill your cup. Find a rest stop, take a deep breath, and give yourself a break.

You deserve it. Period!

Journal Prompts
What does rejuvenate mean to me?

How can you break out of your routine and infuse your days with new experiences that nourish your well-being?

_____
_____
_____
_____

Where are you on this journey, and how can you navigate this unfamiliar territory with self-compassion and understanding?

_____
_____
_____
_____

Assess how your loss is influencing you. Is it actively guiding your actions, or do you feel overwhelmed by its direction?

_____
_____
_____
_____
_____

Reflect on your emotions and explore their depths to understand better and manage them. How can you create a safe and nurturing space for this emotional journey?

_____
_____
_____
_____
_____

Exercise

- Reflect on your journey through grief, noting the significant moments and emotions you have experienced.

- Identify the stages of grief you have encountered, disregarding the limitations of the traditional '5 Stages of Grief.'

- How has each one shaped and transformed you and helped you embrace the uniqueness of your grief process?

- Use your insights to create a personalized map of your grief journey, honoring your path of healing and growth.

A Note of Love:
Create a New Path of Navigation

You know where you are now, which leads us to the question:

Where do you want to be?

When navigating your grief, there's no right way to approach it. Whether finding a hidden path, creating a secret tunnel, or taking a scenic route, options are available. What's important is figuring out how you want the experience to feel and look. Remember, you have the power to reroute your journey through grief.

It's important to follow your heart and pursue what you truly desire. There's no need to hold on to sadness and view it as a burden, a curse, or a punishment.

Consider using the 7 Stages as a guide. Transform your discomfort into significance by focusing on what you need right now.

Discover a new route for navigation that revitalizes and refreshes you. A path that allows you to rest, mourn, grieve, and savor all at once.

That's what our angels want for us. That's what your angel wants for you. May they guide and lift you to your new journey ahead.

Journal Prompts

Where do you envision yourself on your grief journey, and what steps can you take to navigate toward that destination with purpose and intention?

_____
_____
_____

How can you embrace the freedom to choose your path through grief, discover hidden routes, create new ones, or take a scenic and healing approach?

_____
_____
_____

What desires and aspirations in your heart can propel you forward, empowering you to let go of burdensome emotions and embrace the transformative power of grief?

_____
_____
_____

How can you use the 7 Stages to find significance and growth within discomfort, allowing you to focus on what you need for healing?

_____
_____
_____

In your quest for a revitalizing and refreshing route, how can you create space to rest, mourn, grieve, and savor all the different aspects of your experience, honoring the guidance of your angels on this new path of discovery?

_____
_____
_____

Vision Board Exercise

Incorporate these prompts into your vision board. The vision board serves as a daily reminder of the path you want to take, helping to keep you focused, motivated, and aligned with your intentions for healing and growth.

- Envision Your Destination: Imagine where you want to be on your grief journey.

- Explore New Paths: Discover alternative ways to navigate grief and find solace.

- Follow Your Heart: Pursue joy and healing without holding on to sadness.

- Design Your Route: Create a personalized roadmap for healing and self-care.

Honoring Our Loved Ones

OBJECTIVE:

To explore the power of not just moving with your grief but leaping forward with it!

A Note of Love:
Leaping Into Your Next Level

We've talked all about moving with your grief. But let's not stop there.

One of the most rejuvenating ways to honor your loved one is by living your life to the fullest. Pursue your dreams, take action, and accomplish that one thing you always discussed with them. Let your love for your angel fuel a new passion.

Grief has the potential to awaken us if we let it. It reminds us of what is truly important and can provide us with clarity, emotions, and spiritual guidance to assist us in rejuvenating.

For you, that jump could mean launching the business you've always wanted to start. Perhaps it's mentoring, coaching, or assisting someone in your circumstance. Relocating to the beach, the country, or the city

Writing a book, buying a house, or taking that dream vacation.
Or maybe it's starting therapy and prioritizing self-care.

You know, that next-level version of you. Honor your loved ones by leaping to the next level in their honor!

Do something outside the box. Do something you'd never considered before—your next level is waiting!

Journal Prompts

What dream have you always shared with your loved one, and how can you take action to pursue it now, letting their love fuel your passion?

_____
_____
_____

Grief has the potential to awaken us to what truly matters; what newfound clarity, emotion, or spiritual guidance can you use to rejuvenate and take a leap forward in your life?

_____
_____
_____

Think about the possibilities: launching that long-dreamed business, mentoring others, moving to a new place, writing a book, or taking a dream vacation - which next-level leap feels right for you to honor your loved one's memory?

_____
_____
_____

Challenge yourself to do something bold and out of the box, something you'd never considered before; what action can you take to leap to the next level and embrace the life that honors your loved one powerfully?

_____
_____
_____

Vision Board Exercise

- Gather magazines, images, and quotes representing the 'next-level' version of yourself and the life you want to live in honor of your loved one.

- Select pictures that inspire you to start your mornings with joy, embrace each day with purpose, and infuse your daily life with passion and fulfillment.

- Include visuals that symbolize the kind of work you want to do, whether starting a business, mentoring others, or pursuing a career that brings you fulfillment.

- Find images that depict how you envision your rest and play, whether traveling to new places, enjoying hobbies, or spending quality time with loved ones.

- Choose pictures representing the type of place you want to live, whether it's a peaceful countryside retreat, a bustling city apartment, or a cozy beachside home.

- Assemble the images, quotes, and visuals on a vision board, arranging them in a way that sparks joy and inspiration. Display your vision board in a place where you can see it daily, allowing it to remind you of the leap you're taking to live your life to the fullest in honor of your loved one.

A Note of Love:
Explore the World to Explore Your World

In the last chapter, we mapped out your new grief navigation. Now, it's time to head to a destination unknown!

Traveling is one of the most powerful ways to shift to your next level. You are traveling, intending to leap!

Remember: We're not just moving with your grief. We're taking a leap you've never thought of before.

For example, you might do something or go somewhere your loved one would never imagine you doing but would be amazed and inspired to see.

Going to Coachella. Reigniting your magic in the Sedona desert, sinking into the Canary Islands sand, exploring the quiet of the Colorado mountains, or finding yourself in the city's vibrance.

Have you ever traveled to a destination in sync with your desired energy? This is where the healing begins for all my grief warriors.

This is why I offer 1:1 retreats: Destination Unknown. These leaps form a transformative path for warriors to explore themselves. It's mystically explosive, whether recovering from loss, trauma, suicide, or abuse.

What a JOY it would be to revitalize our healing spirits!

Journal Prompts

Have you ever imagined yourself in a destination that perfectly aligns with your desired energy? A place where you feel connected to your loved one's spirit?
Where will your leap of healing take you?

_____
_____
_____

What bold step can you take to honor your loved one and inspire yourself? Embrace the unknown and discover new possibilities on your journey.

_____
_____
_____

Are you ready to revitalize your healing spirit? What does a "Destination Unknown" retreat look like to you? (location, days, season, theme)

_____
_____
_____

Honoring Our Emotions

OBJECTIVE:

To honor our emotions by embracing the present, permitting ourselves to rest, and discovering a new perspective.

A Note of Love:
Giving Your Emotions Permission to Just... Exist!

Lack of motivation has nothing to do with having poor days or experiencing uncomfortable feelings. Our resilience in the face of pain's how we cope when things go wrong.

Feelings can't be judged as "good" or "bad." Feeling and healing through emotions does not need you to convince yourself there is a "right" or "wrong" way to feel.

Because they are uniquely yours, only you can adequately respect your feelings. I will not try to persuade you there is one way to improve.

But I will tell you that we recover more quickly when celebrating rather than punishing our feelings. We may provide the solace and care they require by welcoming and accommodating them.

Giving yourself to your feelings gives you the strength and insight to decide whether to let them in or out. Allow your sadness to be there. It is good, from a few weeks to several years.

Allow yourself to relax and give up fighting. Renew. Rejuvenate. Consider it your "emotional PTO" (Paid Time Off). Stop with the forced laughter and "should ofs."

Journal Prompts

How do you typically react to your bad days and painful emotions? Reflect on your immediate responses and whether they involve resistance or acceptance.

_____
_____
_____

Are there any emotions you tend to suppress or judge as "bad"? Why do you think you react this way, and how might it affect your well-being?

_____
_____
_____

Imagine giving yourself emotional PTO (Paid Time Off) to resist your feelings. Think about a recent challenging experience or a "poor day." How did you cope with it and show compassion during that time?

_____
_____
_____

Exercise

- Take some time to locate a serene spot and explore your emotional terrain.

- Visualize your feelings as weather patterns: storms, fog, clouds, sunshine, rainbows, snowfall, or winds. Recognize that these emotions are neither good nor bad -- check in with your emotional weather report.

- Now, instead of trying to alter the weather, envision yourself donning rain boots and stepping outside. Embrace the clouds' shapes, the fog's enigma, or the comfort in the cold.

- Adapt and flow with the emotional weather you're experiencing rather than pushing against it. Allow yourself to adjust and find the beauty in each emotional climate.

A Note of Love:
Honoring Your Grief Emotions in a New Light

There are beautiful ways to honor every shade, shape, and sheen of emotion. There is something magical about honoring your grief in a new light rather than alone in the dark. Again, there is no right or wrong way, but I hope you can look at it in a new light today.

However, you're feeling. Happy or sad. Angry or annoyed. Hopeful or confused. It's valid -- and I want you to see that more rejuvenatingly.

Channel that emotion of writing a poem, starting a painting, or creating something new!

Do something you and your angel loved to do together. Listen to their favorite music, read their favorite book, or watch their favorite movie! Look at pictures or share your favorite stories about them.

- Go for a walk, or spend a relaxing day inside!
- Honor an old tradition, or start a new one!
- Take a day for yourself, or reach out to old and new friends and loved ones!

There is no right or wrong -- only what's right for you. Connect your grief emotion, whatever it may be, and honor yourself with it.

Emotions mean you care. Caring is often painful -- but I promise, it's one of the most magical things about you. Let your magic rejuvenate your soul.

Journal Prompts

Reflect on a recent emotional experience you had. How did you initially respond to it, and did you feel comfortable embracing that emotion? If not, explore why and how you can honor it moving forward.

_____
_____
_____

Think about a creative outlet that appeals to you (e.g., writing, painting, or crafting). How might you use this outlet to channel and express your emotions in a healing and transformative way?

_____
_____
_____

Recall a cherished memory with your loved one. How can you incorporate elements of that memory into your present life to honor their presence and keep their spirit alive?

_____
_____
_____

Exercise

Create an Emotion Magic Board: On a piece of paper or in a journal, create a visual representation of your emotions using colors, shapes, and words. Each emotion can have its section on the board. As you experience different emotions, add to your magic board to acknowledge and embrace them. Use this board as a reminder that all your emotions are valid and contribute to the beautiful tapestry of your being. Allow your emotions to guide and inspire you with compassion and love as you move through the grief journey.

Kicking Up Your Serotonin

OBJECTIVE:

To understand how you can care for your brain to rejuvenate your body and soul!

A Note of Love:
Give Yourself a Mental Health Boost!

We've mapped out your new grief navigation and envisioned your destination unknown... Now, it's time to fuel your soul for the journey!

Our brains are an ongoing science experiment of chemicals, neurotransmitters, and hormones. Knowing how your brain works can rewire, refuel, and rejuvenate it with excitement, joy, and vibrance! Become the mad scientist of your brain.

This starts with your new best friend, serotonin: the "happy neurotransmitter." It aids our digestive system, sleep patterns, learning, and relationships.

We often talk about how changing your life starts with changing your thoughts. This is true... But sometimes, it's a bit exhausting to think "happy thoughts," especially if you face real, raw grief and trauma.

To help navigate this, you can reframe your thoughts by starting with your actions.

Because serotonin is connected to our lifestyles, we can take aligned ACTIONS to kick up our serotonin, all-natural! Let's boost your mental health: Pick what speaks to YOU best!

FOOD

Self-care is food (which we'll dive into even more in the final"E" of EMBRACE: Eat Healthily!). Most of our serotonin is processed in our guts. You can't eat serotonin, but you can eat "tryptophan," an amino acid that magically turns into serotonin when combined with carbs.

Some serotonin-boosting combos are:
- Salmon + quinoa or brown rice
- Oatmeal + nuts and berries
- Whole wheat turkey sandwich
- Pineapple + yogurt
- Eggs + toast
- Cheese + nuts (charcuterie board, anyone?)

MOVEMENT

Runner's high is real, as aerobic exercises stimulate blood pumping and serotonin.

Find your favorite way to move, whether walking or hiking in nature, swimming in the pool or ocean, taking an aerobic class, or even dancing around in your kitchen!

SUNLIGHT

Sunshine is Mother Nature's natural medicine. Just 10-15 minutes of pure sunshine elevates our moods and warms our souls.

Remind yourself of the beauty around you with just a few minutes outside each day, whether rainy or cloudy.

MASSAGE

This is your excuse to book the massage. Your body and brain deserve the rejuvenation.

Massages leave our bodies feeling more relaxed and rejuvenated by releasing stress chemicals and pumping up our happy ones.

SLEEP

Take a nap. I mean it!

Sleep is anything but lazy. It sharpens your mind, uplifts your heart, and recharges your body. A 20-minute nap can act as a reset button, while a 10-minute nap can boost your spirits.

Permit yourself to rest -- add a nap to your to-do list.

Journal Prompts

Reflect on a recent day when you experienced a surge of happiness and contentment. What activities or actions were you engaged in during that day?

_____
_____
_____

How can you incorporate more of these activities into your daily life to promote a positive mindset and elevate your serotonin levels naturally?

_____
_____
_____

Explore the connection between your emotions and your lifestyle choices. Are there any habits or behaviors that may be hindering your serotonin production? How can you replace these with healthier, mood-boosting alternatives?

_____
_____
_____

Create a list of activities you've always wanted to try but have not explored. Choose one from the list and commit to trying it within the next week. How does stepping out of your comfort zone and trying something new align with your journey to refuel your soul?

_____
_____
_____

Remember, you have the power to rewire and rejuvenate your brain through intentional actions and lifestyle choices. Embrace the journey of becoming the mad scientist of your brain and fuel your soul for a transformative and uplifting experience!

Exercise

Choose one of the five serotonin-boosting activities and do it!

Eat serotonin-supportive foods!

Move your body in a fun, refreshing way!

Get some sunlight!

Book a massage!

Take a nap!

Exploring New, High-Vibe Routes of Rejuvenation

OBJECTIVE:

To explore your not-so-typical kinds of rejuvenation to open your mind, body, and spirit to next-level healing.

A Note of Love:
Your Next Level is on a Whole New Level!

Remember: To leap into your next level, you've got to make next-level moves. You know that next-level version of you -- your higher self.

Sometimes, you've just got to ask yourself, "What would my higher self do?"

Doing that one thing and taking that trip can shift your reality and give you your power back. But continually exploring new, high-vibe routes of rejuvenation can constantly put you in place to RECEIVE your healing.

New experiences open your heart, mind, and soul to the Universe to receive more. It's not just about raising vibrations but showing yourself that you can try new things.

It proves to you that healing isn't linear. No two paths look the same. (and thank goodness for that!)

So today, I want you to do something different. Something out of the box. Depending on who you are, it might be as simple as going out on a Tuesday or staying in on a Friday.

Do something new for yourself! Imagine what the most aligned, high-vibe version of you would do today -- and do it with her.

Journal Prompts

Take a moment to connect with your higher self, the version of you that embodies confidence and alignment. Ask yourself, "What does my higher self truly desire now?" Listen to the whispers of your intuition and write down any insights or inspirations that come to mind.

_____
_____
_____

Reflect on a time when you tried something new or stepped outside of your comfort zone. How did that experience make you feel? What did you learn about yourself in the process? How can you use this knowledge to continue exploring new, high-vibe routes of rejuvenation in your life?

_____
_____
_____

Visualize yourself spending a day with your higher self, engaging in activities that bring joy, fulfillment, and healing. Write a detailed journal entry describing this day, from morning to evening. How does immersing yourself in the energy of your higher self impact your overall well-being and sense of empowerment?

_____
_____
_____

Exercise

Plan and execute a "High-Vibe Day" for yourself.

- Choose a day of the week that feels significant, or pick a day that works for you. Fill your day with activities that resonate with your higher self's desires and aspirations. It could be trying a new hobby, visiting a place you've never been, indulging in self-care rituals, or spending time in nature.

- Throughout the day, be mindful of how each experience makes you feel and its impact on your emotional state. At the end of the day, journal about your "High-Vibe Day" experience and any insights you gained from embodying your higher self's energy.

- Embrace the magic of trying something different and allow yourself to receive the healing and transformation that comes with stepping into your next-level self.

A Note of Love:
Exploring High-Frequency Ways to Hit 'Refresh'

Rejuvenation is the soul's refresh option. Let's hit the refresh button in a new way today!

Woooo weeee! We've discussed everyday self-care moves, like naps, walks, massages, and sunshine. Now, let's think out of the box, give our healing journeys, and use high-vibe healing methods to give our healing journeys the transformative transformation we seek. Let's examine a few of my favorites:

Hyperbaric Chambers

Our bodies heal themselves. Sometimes, we're left with scars that remind us of what we've overcome. They tie us to our past while letting us move forward with our wounds.

Our bodies use oxygen to heal our wounds. It moves and flows through our blood, carrying it to areas needing healing. Oxygen has intuitive, adaptable energy (like our air element friends)! It's the same with mental, emotional, and spiritual wounds.

Hyperbaric Chambers ramp up this healing by increasing the oxygen given to your body, giving the energy needed for our tissue and cells to recover faster. Spending time in a hyperbaric chamber can rejuvenate your mind and body with the dynamic healing energy it needs.

Blood-Spinning Machine

We're still thinking out of the park, so stick with me! Blood spinning (or PRP therapy) injects your healing powers back into your own body.

A practitioner will take a sample of your blood and put it in a centrifuge that separates it into components. They'll inject your platelet-rich plasma into an area that needs healing to concentrate your recovery, helping your body heal.

IV Drips

Your body's healing energy runs through your veins. But sometimes, this energy gets stuck. Blocked. Deprived of what it needs to flow and rejuvenate.

If you've neglected your body for some time, you might consider IV drips. You can inject healing into your bloodstream, quickly delivering healing and nutrients through your veins!

There are drips for hydration, immunity, energy, recovery, and restoration!

Infrared Red Saunas

Trauma can send our souls off-balance. This misalignment of our yin and yang is deeply tied to our bodies' temperature. Yang is your fire energy, centered on action, movement, and growth. Yin is your cold, damp point centered on rest and restoration. When either depleted or overextended, we need to refine our balance.

Infrared saunas can ignite our yang energy, boosting our serotonin, reducing stress, and empowering focus and strength.

Pay attention to the energy you need. What needs to be balanced? Major life events can shift us from alignment, making us feel less and less like ourselves. But tuning into our needs -- focusing on how we can care for ourselves -- leads us back to our center.

Take a giant, rejuvenating leap toward your aligned, higher self today!

Journal Prompts

What HYPER WELLNESS service would you include to align with your higher self's desires and aspirations?
_____
_____
_____

Write a detailed itinerary for this special day, outlining each experience you plan to indulge in.
_____
_____
_____

How do these experiences resonate with your soul? How do you expect each activity to impact your emotional state and overall well-being?
_____
_____
_____

On your "High-Vibe Day," be present and mindful. Take note of changes in your energy, mood, and perspective. Afterward, write down your experiences and insights gained on this healing journey.
_____
_____
_____

Exercise

- Create a "High-Vibe Healing Menu" for yourself, featuring a variety of out-of-the-box healing methods and activities.
- Include options like trying a new holistic therapy, exploring sound healing, journaling with affirmations, meditating in nature, or practicing breathwork exercises.
- Over the next week, experiment with different items from your menu and keep a healing journal to document your experiences, emotions, and any profound shifts you notice.
- At the end of the week, reflect on how these high-vibe healing methods have impacted your overall well-being and rejuvenation journey.
- Embrace the transformative power of trying something new and invite in the magic of healing on a deeper level.

Your Journey, Our Gratitude

Healing doesn't reside in the ceaseless whirlwind of daily life; it finds its home in moments of stillness.

Whether in quiet reflection or much-needed naps, the path to your well-being has already been laid out by your own hands. Now, the compass is in your grasp: your next destination is entirely your call.

Are you content to linger where you are, finding solace in rest and rejuvenation? That's absolutely okay.

Do you feel compelled to move, charting new landscapes of self-discovery? Equally valid.

Healing doesn't adhere to a straight line. It zigzags, it loops, it retraces its steps and then surges forward anew. It's a web of complexity, but it's within that intricate maze that we form a truce with our grief.

Remember that self-care isn't a luxury; it's your right. It's your way of inscribing grief within your narrative of triumph, honoring not just those we've lost but also celebrating the one who remains—you. So go on, extend to yourself the grace of healing and the gift of joy; if anyone is deserving of it, it's you.

With Infinite Intention

The Grief Warrior

AWAKEN
The Fifth Stage of Grief

EMBRACE

MICHELE C. BELL
THE GRIEF WARRIOR®

you've made it

EMBRACE the voyage into our fifth stage:

— *awaken* —

Welcome to a realm where words are not just symbols but alchemical elements designed to transmute your very existence. What you're about to delve into isn't just prose; it's an orchestrated cosmos folded into the fibers of the mundane. Each phrase you encounter is a pivot—imbued with purpose, meant to touch the ineffable while simultaneously shaping your palpable reality.

"To awaken is not merely to observe reality; it's an existential plunge into the depths of our being, a baptism by life's fires that heralds authentic metamorphosis."

Are you prepared to unfold your next chapter, an existential waltz guided by the compass of intuitive wisdom?

Table of Contents

Namaste 03
Instructions 04
Lesson One: Emotional Imagery 05
Lesson Two: The Power of Visionary Manifestations 13
Lesson Three: Connect to Your Source Energy 21
Lesson Four: Becoming Nobody 29
Lesson Five: Impermanence 36
Lesson Six: The Path to Enlightenment 42

NAMASTE
it's time to wake up

Let's begin this enlightening journey with a POD meditation to help us set a purposeful intention for our minds, bodies, and spirits.

**This is your "Go To" Breathwork POD Meditation
throughout this lesson - revisit this page after each lesson.
(PAUSE OBSERVE DISCERN)**

Find Your Breath, Find Your Center

Begin by settling into a position that encourages both relaxation and alignment. Let your body be fully supported as you close your eyes and shift your focus inward.

Inhale through your nose, deep enough to feel your abdomen rise, filling you with life-giving air. Then, slowly exhale through your lips, releasing any lingering tension or preoccupations. How does that feel?

With each breath, anchor yourself in the immediate now, allowing the present to be your sanctuary.

Next, gently steer your attention to your heart's center. Visualize a soft, luminous light glowing from within, casting a warm embrace around your entire self. As you continue breathing, can you feel its radiance intensifying, infused with love, courage, and self-belief?

As you breathe out, allow this exercise to become a mental sweep, clearing away distractions or anxieties and making room for focus and wisdom. What thoughts or concerns are you willing to release?

Pause here to appreciate your inherent potential. In the rhythm of your breath, reconnect with your unique qualities and strengths. Can you sense an alignment, a symbiosis, between your talents and confidence? Believe in your capability to make a meaningful impact on both your life and the lives of those you touch.

When you sense it's time, gradually open your eyes, but hold onto this enriched state of mind. Your breath isn't just a biological necessity; it's your gateway to self-exploration and metamorphosis.

As you step back into the world, know that this mindful breathing practice is always available, a wellspring of inner clarity and balance. How might you carry this practice into the rest of your day?

So, as you transition back into your surroundings, take these moments of inner peace with you. Whenever life gets overwhelming, remember that your breath is always there: a faithful companion in your journey of self-discovery.

INSTRUCTIONS
for awaken exercises

Starting your day with a connection to your inner spirit is essential, and I'm here to help you achieve that. Our exercises will begin between 4-6 a.m., during the peaceful and tranquil morning hours. These hours are vital as they allow us to be present in the moment and listen to our inner guidance, free of distractions and noise. Let's tune in and silence our thoughts to hear what our source energy tells us.

Let's start by going through each section's journal prompts and then move on to practicing the Awaken breathwork meditation. This meditation is a way to enhance our grace, divinity, and mindfulness. Let's consider it a ritual.

Consider creating a peaceful space in nature for your Awaken exercise! You could opt for your patio, backyard, or even your room with an open window. The key is selecting a location that allows you to awaken purposefully.

To start your practice, stand up and take off your shoes. Connect with the Earth or floor by noticing the cool tile, warm rug, solid concrete, or soft grass under your feet.

Before you start your Awaken meditation, please get comfortable and fully awake for a few minutes. When you feel prepared, you may begin the meditation.

LESSON ONE

Emotional Imagery:
Feel That it's REAL

Objective:

To explore the power of emotional imagery
and turn our visions into reality.

A Note of Love:
Reawakening Your Inner Child's Imagination

When was the last time you spent time with your inner child?

Take a pause. Let's connect with that eternally young, vulnerable, and curious facet of you—the inner child. What are they whispering to you today? Could it be a yearning for spontaneity, a call for audacious exploration, or a nudge toward joyful liberation?

As we journey through the years, it's easy to let the wonders of imagination fade into the background. But what if we make it a priority instead? After all, the power to journey through imagined lands and untangle complex realities is a gift that begs to be nurtured and celebrated. How are you nourishing your imagination today?

Your imagination isn't just a whimsical escape; it's a therapeutic powerhouse. Visualization, after all, is a core component of how many of us meditate and manifest. Can you feel how it is deeply woven into your emotional tapestry, forming a unique access point to empathy and creativity?

Imagination is your bridge from the abstract universe of your mind to the tactile world around you. Be it the vivid hues of a sunflower or the surreal whimsy of a red and orange striped elephant donning a top hat—what unrealities are you willing to make real today?

The arena of your mind is fertile ground. Whether you're cultivating sunflowers or striped elephants, remember that your imagination is a realm where anything is possible. So, what are you going to bring to life next?

A Note of Love:
Reawakening Your Inner Child's Imagination

Have you ever paused to dwell on the palpable texture of excitement? It might manifest as a flutter in your stomach, reminiscent of rollercoasters, pulsing crowds, or breathtaking landscapes.

How often do we invoke this emotional cinema when we engage with art forms like music and movies? A horror film might stir a primal fear despite being securely tucked in bed. Contrastingly, a catchy pop tune might turn your kitchen into a dance floor.

So, what's the secret sauce here?

Your imagination doesn't just create; it feels, making your experiences phenomenally real. It is a catalyst for emotional excavation and self-discovery. Can you think of the last time you tapped into this unrealized source of therapeutic creativity?

Now, let's pivot. Close your eyes for a moment and retreat to a place of peace that you've experienced or yearned for. Maybe it's a sunlit beach, the reassuring laughter of people you love, or the solitary joy of a book that speaks your soul. As you visualize, can you also hear it? The rhythmic pounding of waves, the harmonious laughter, or the music that touches your core?

Stay there. Let yourself absorb the saltiness of the ocean air, the warmth of meaningful connection, or the relaxation flowing through your muscles during a massage. Isn't it remarkable how you can summon such tranquility?

Ever ponder what 'peace' really feels like to you? Could it be a sigh of relief, the absence of fear, or perhaps a steady, comforting heartbeat?

Journal Prompts

Answer each prompt with at least 2-3 paragraphs. Give yourself time and space to ask these questions, explore ideas, and use your imagination to answer.

When was the last time you spent quality time with your inner child? What activities can you do to reconnect with their sense of play, adventure, and curiosity?

How does your imagination impact your emotional experiences? Take a moment to reflect on a memory or image that evokes a specific emotion and explore the sensations it brings.

_____
_____
_____
_____
_____
_____
_____
_____
_____
_____
_____
_____
_____
_____
_____
_____
_____

What sentiment is currently taking hold of me? How is this particular emotion sparking the liveliness of my inner child?

_____
_____
_____
_____
_____
_____
_____
_____
_____
_____
_____
_____
_____
_____
_____

In what ways do you use your imagination as a therapeutic tool? How can you incorporate visualization and emotional connection to enhance your meditations and manifestations?

_____
_____
_____
_____
_____
_____
_____
_____
_____
_____
_____
_____
_____
_____
_____
_____
_____
_____
_____
_____

Take a mental journey to a peaceful place or memory. Close your eyes and fully immerse yourself in the experience. What sights, sounds, and sensations do you encounter? How does this moment of peace make you feel?

_____
_____
_____
_____
_____

Reflect on the beauty of sound and its ability to bring tranquility. Visualize the sounds of crashing waves, laughter, or your favorite melody filling your ears. How can you embrace the calming power of sound in your daily life?

_____
_____
_____
_____
_____

Exercise

Begin your AWAKEN exercise between 4-6 a.m.

Find your Awakening space.

Start standing, and ground your bare feet into the Earth or floor beneath you.

When you're ready, practice the Awaken Breathwork Meditation.

LESSON TWO

The Power of Visionary Manifestations:
Energy Manipulation

Objective:

To understand the power of visionary manifestations and manipulate your energy to align with your intentions.

A Note of Love:
Awaken Your Inner Visionary

Awaken is not merely a term but an imperative—a call to inner rebellion against the mundane sediments of existence. It embodies more than wellness; it is a Radical Embrace, a tango with the universe within, where self-expression becomes an act of mindfulness, meditation a political rebellion, and revitalization the nourishment of the soul's perpetual becoming.

Let's dispense with the pedestrian idea that visionaries only come in the guise of industrial magnates or cinematic magicians. A visionary dares to tear through the commonplace fabric to glimpse the ineffable patterns beyond. It's not about inspiration; it's about existential alchemy.

My narrative—stitched with the golden thread of LifePath 11, the chaotic dance of a Heyoka Empath, and the celestial mechanics of a Manifesting Generator—is a single testament in the sacred text of *Being*. Challenges and triumphs are not episodes but stanzas in an eternal poem.

The retreats to Unknown Destinations I offer are neither escapes nor vacations; they're pilgrimages into the soul's labyrinth. You're not a mere participant but a co-conspirator in crafting a bespoke tapestry of transformational modalities. In this intimate crucible, we will stir the pot of your inner wisdom, crystallize insights from the brine of your experience, and unleash the torrent of your creative potential—your brand of cosmic sorcery.

In this sanctum, the alchemy of visionary manifestation isn't a mere outcome; it's the ink with which we rewrite the script of your existence. Each new perspective is a fresh verse in your life's sonnet, each growth spurt a new brushstroke on your existential canvas, and each moment of self-discovery a cosmic note in your lifelong symphony.

A Note of Love:
Awaken Your Inner Visionary

Are You Not More Than a Cosmic Accident?
You find yourself standing on the precipice of potential, the edge of existential inquiry. But before you dive into the celestial waters, dare to carve a sanctuary within your psyche. This is the hallowed ground upon which your connection to the ineffable—be it God, angels, or the raw pulsations of the universe—will be forged. Call it the Alchemist's workshop of the soul, where leaden thoughts transmute into golden wisdom.

Cryptic Dispatches from the Beyond
The world is rife with signs—encrypted messages longing to be deciphered. Do you recognize them? These are not mere coincidences but intimate correspondences from your higher self or source energy. Disconnect from the clamor of existential chaos and listen. To do this, one must adopt a Wittgensteinian lens, understanding that the boundaries of your world are set not merely by language but by attentiveness to the signposts of life itself.

The Will to Elevate
Personal elevation is not a frivolous want but a Nietzschean imperative—a Will to Power of the spirit. To vibrate higher is to shed the cumbersome weight of your earthly limitations. Immerse yourself in atmospheres and energies that are conducive to this divine rebellion. Surround yourself with beings, locations, and endeavors that are inspiring and almost electrifying in their transformative charge.

The Riddle of Being and Becoming
So, what then? Is the journey complete? Of course not. The paradox of existence is that the moment you claim to "Be," you inevitably become a relic of your becoming. As Ram Dass would counsel, focus on the "here and now," the eternal present where being and becoming dance in cosmic harmony.

"In the labyrinth of existence, we are all both seeker and oracle, question and answer fused in cosmic dialogue. May you find not mere paths but dimensions, where every turn is a revelation and every pause a poem unto itself."

Journal Prompts

Answer each prompt with at least 2-3 paragraphs. Give yourself time and space to ask these questions, explore ideas, and use your imagination to answer.

Reflect on your inner journey and the growth you've experienced through the practice of EMBRACE. How have intentional self-expression, mindfulness, and meditation influenced your path as a visionary?

Who are the visionaries you look up to, and what specific qualities or characteristics do they possess that inspire you? How can you incorporate some of these qualities into your own life to awaken your inner visionary?

_____
_____
_____
_____
_____
_____
_____
_____
_____
_____
_____
_____
_____
_____
_____
_____
_____
_____
_____

Explore the challenges and achievements that have shaped your unique life journey. How have these experiences contributed to your ability to embrace visionary manifestations and navigate life's blessings and obstacles?

_____
_____
_____
_____
_____
_____
_____
_____
_____
_____
_____
_____
_____
_____

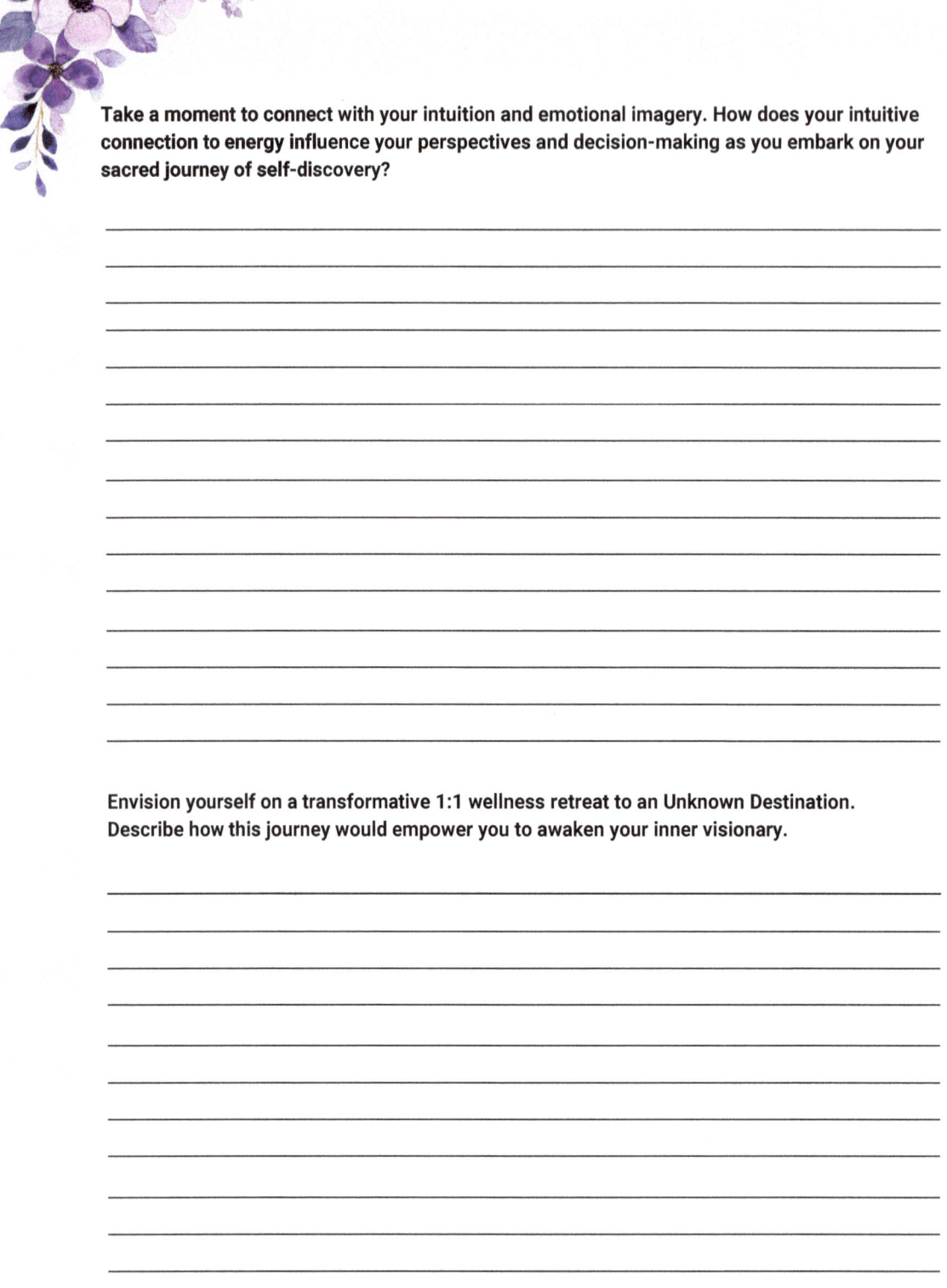

Take a moment to connect with your intuition and emotional imagery. How does your intuitive connection to energy influence your perspectives and decision-making as you embark on your sacred journey of self-discovery?

_____
_____
_____
_____
_____
_____
_____
_____
_____
_____
_____
_____
_____
_____
_____
_____
_____
_____
_____

Envision yourself on a transformative 1:1 wellness retreat to an Unknown Destination. Describe how this journey would empower you to awaken your inner visionary.

_____
_____
_____
_____
_____
_____
_____
_____
_____
_____
_____
_____
_____
_____

Exercise

Begin your exercise between 4-6 a.m.

Find your Awakening space.

Start in a standing position, and ground your bare feet into the Earth or floor beneath you.

When you're ready, practice the Awaken Breathwork Meditation.

A Note of Love:
What is Your Purpose?

Soul Seat: Imagine your hand gently resting upon your Tan Tien, that secret cauldron of vitality near your navel. Elevate your other hand to your Soul Seat—the sanctuary perched between the heart's labyrinth and the voice's altar. Picture an ethereal filament tethering these two realms, pulsating with the essence of your 'why,' the primordial yearning sculpting your existential architecture.

Individuation Nexus: The term "individuation" whispers its legacy from Latin—a tongue ancient as the concept itself. "Individuus," a sentinel guarding the notion of the "indivisible." As you traverse the eldritch corridors of soul retrieval, seize the paradox of Becoming Nobody. In this existential vacuum, your boundless potential shall echo back to you, revealing fragments of your reclaimed soul.

The Hara Continuum is not just a line but a cosmic string, a trinity of nodal points linking you to the cosmic loom of existence. It's your umbilical cord to the source, your North Star guiding you to purpose, and your anchor tethering you to Earthly reality. It's the axis upon which your universe spins.

Misalignment in your Hara Continuum manifests as existential dissonance. A thirst for an unknown 'more,' a descent into the abyss of purposelessness, the haunting specter of aloneness. Yet, alignment metamorphoses this disarray into rooted certitude. You no longer hunger for external validation; you sup on existential authenticity.

Your Soul Seat—your existential epicenter—radiates increasingly vivid luminosity as you forge connections skyward through your Individuation Nexus and earthward through your Tan Tien.

In the cosmic ballet, purpose isn't found—it's woven. Align your inner stars, and 'what you seek' becomes 'what you are.'

Journal Prompts

Answer each prompt with at least 2-3 paragraphs. Give yourself time and space to ask these questions, explore ideas, and use your imagination to answer.

Take a few deep breaths and place your hand on your Tan Tien, then slowly raise the other hand to your Soul Seat. Close your eyes and visualize the connection between these points. What does this connection represent to you? How does it relate to your aspirations and inner perception?

Reflect on the concept of "individuation" and what it means to you. How have external factors influenced your sense of self in the past? How can embracing Becoming Nobody help you reclaim your authentic essence and tap into your untapped potential?

___

Consider the Hara Line and its significance in connecting you to your source energy, purpose, and the Earth and Heavens. How do you feel grounded and centered when aligned with your Hara Line? How does this alignment affect your overall sense of well-being and inner strength?

___

Think about a time when your Hara Line felt out of alignment. How did it manifest in your life? What were the challenges you faced during that period? How did you work towards realigning with your purpose and source power?

_____
_____
_____
_____
_____
_____

Imagine your purpose and Soul Seat growing brighter as you strengthen your connection with Mother Earth. What steps can you take to nurture this alignment and fully embrace your soul's purpose? How will this transformation impact other aspects of your life, relationships, and personal growth journey?

_____
_____
_____
_____
_____
_____

Exercise

Begin your exercise between 4-6 a.m.

Find your Awakening space.

Start in a standing position, and ground your bare feet into the Earth or floor beneath you.

When you're ready, practice the Awaken Breathwork Meditation.

LESSON FOUR

Becoming Nobody

Objective:

To surrender our egos to free ourselves from the regrets, demands, and pressure of the past and future to "be here now."

A Note of Love:
What is Your Purpose?

In the vast cosmic theater, the ultimate role isn't to star as 'Somebody.' It's to artfully vanish into 'Nobody,' where purpose isn't scripted but arises from the ineffable dialogue between one's essence and the universe.

The Weltanschauung peddled by society often dictates: 'Ascend the pedestal of fame to cast a shadow.' Such a myopic lens, isn't it? True gravitas, that seismic resonance, emanates not from the gallery's applause but from the quiet alchemy of inner harmony.

In the theater of existence, consider the radical act of Becoming Nobody. Here, unshackled by the gargantuan ego and societal mirages, your singular essence transcends into a universal chorus. The quest shifts—from the banal vanity of 'becoming somebody' to the sublime serenity of an existential metamorphosis, one that embraces a pulsating oneness with the cosmic lattice.

When you cease to ornament your existence with the detritus of 'shoulds' and 'could haves,' the here and now crystallizes into a sanctuary. It's a cathedral where the hymns are your ever-evolving breaths, thoughts, and very being. Serving, passion, existence—these are the liturgies that transmute 'enough' into plenitude.

Much like Ram Dass's musings on mortality—the untying of life's 'tight shoe' as neither tragedy nor epilogue but a poignant stanza in the ballad of being. Death isn't a realm for a Death Doula but a poetic verse for an Ascension Shaman like me.

Final thought? Pivot with intent. EMBRACE to transcend. Transmute grief into grace—a celestial choreography where every step is purpose incarnate.

> *"Death, not an end, but a threshold—*
> *A door to dimensions yet unseen.*
> *In becoming nobody, we inherit the cosmos,*
> *Life's greatest, yet most elusive scene."* Ram Dass

The Power of The POD:
Unlocking Inner Wisdom through Pause Observation and Discernment

The POD—is more than an acronym; it's a pilgrimage to 'Non-being,' an odyssey beyond the ego.

PAUSE: It's not mere stillness; it's a resolute cessation from the world's ceaseless chatter, a mutiny against distraction. In this sacred void, you unhinge the masks, unraveling the Gordian knots of outward identity. The quietude is not an absence but a potent space—infused with potentialities.

OBSERVE: Witness, don't just see. This stage isn't passive watching; it actively decouples from societal narratives and self-constructed fiction. It's a lucid awareness, devoid of judgment, where you dissect your programmed ideologies, your conceptual wardrobe. What remains is not the fabricated 'you' but a distilled essence—a noumenal self beyond societal contours.

DISCERNMENT: This is your existential compass, your soul's barometer. It transcends mere choice; it's an alignment—a magnetic pull toward what genuinely resonates with your innermost frequencies. It dissolves the validation quest, defying societal yardsticks of what counts as a 'life well-lived.'

In traversing the POD pathway, you're not just reaching a destination but dissolving into the journey itself. You're shedding the egoic shell, tearing down the facades of societal validation, and soaring into an existence not confined by nouns or adjectives. You're not becoming a better version of yourself; you're becoming 'Nobody,' which paradoxically makes you a universal 'Somebody.'

That is the crux—through POD, you unearth existential freedom, liberating you from identities to unite with your most unadulterated Self. Here, you touch the intangible—your indefinable purpose, and from this space, you cease to be a mere role and become a cosmic force.

"In the stillness of pause, the wisdom of observation meets the clarity of discernment, illuminating the path to authentic purpose."

Journal Prompts

Answer each prompt with at least 2-3 paragraphs. Give yourself time and space to ask these questions, explore ideas, and use your imagination to answer.

Pause and Reflect: Take a moment of quietude each day to cultivate space for self-contemplation. How does this practice of the POD help you disengage from external distractions and connect with your authentic self?

___
___
___
___
___
___
___
___
___
___
___
___
___
___
___
___
___
___
___
___
___
___
___
___
___

The Power of Observation: Practice observing your thoughts, feelings, and habits without judgment or criticism. What insights have you gained from this habit of objective observation? How has it impacted your self-concept and sense of purpose?

_____
_____
_____
_____
_____
_____
_____
_____
_____
_____
_____
_____
_____
_____
_____
_____
_____

Embracing Discernment: Listen to the call of your inner sanctuary, intuitive sense, and higher wisdom when making choices. How has discernment guided you to make decisions that resonate with your true self? How does it help you align with your core beliefs and lead a meaningful life?

_____
_____
_____
_____
_____
_____
_____
_____
_____
_____
_____
_____
_____

Unveiling Your Authentic Self: Reflect on the transformative journey of "becoming nobody." How has learning about "The POD" modality allowed you to shed layers of external self-definition and societal pressures? How does living from a place of inner harmony enable you to recognize and embrace your authentic self fully?

_____
_____
_____
_____
_____
_____
_____
_____
_____
_____
_____
_____
_____
_____
_____

Exercise

Begin your exercise between 4-6 a.m.

Find your Awakening space.

Start in a standing position, and ground your bare feet into the Earth or floor beneath you.

When you're ready, practice the Awaken Breathwork Meditation.

LESSON FIVE

Impermanence:
Life's Great Wake-Up Call

Objective:

To embrace the beauty of impermanence
and begin to live our lives to the fullest.

A Note of Love:
Nothing Is Permanent
(and that's okay)

Embracing Impermanence

In the theater of fleeting time,
Where Change pens each unfolding rhyme,
We dance between the here and gone
A twilight kiss, a breaking dawn.

Why dread the falling of the leaf,
When autumn paints, its bold relief?
Or mourn the melting of the snow,
When spring's first buds have room to grow?

Each ending whispers to us, "See,
You're but a fleeting melody."
In impermanence, we find
The sacred hymns of humankind.

So let us meet each shifting tide,
No longer seeking place to hide.
Embrace the Now—our truest home—
And find in Change, we're never alone.

In our obsessive quest for permanence, we forge iron-clad contracts and calcify routines as though we could stave off the inevitable tides of Change—the primordial alchemy of existence. These artifices of control are but sandcastles before the oceanic flux of life; beautiful, yes, but fated to erode.

We hold our breath in ephemeral euphoria, naive to the hurricane of Change that churns in the distance—until it roars ashore, dismantling our mirages.

Ah, don't mistake me for a cynic. Impermanence is not a tragic footnote but the ink with which life is written. It's the leitmotif of our existence, an invitation to dance in the theater of the Now. Each change we lament is but a death, and each death
a doorway—an ethos deeply etched in the cyclical philosophies of Buddhism.

When you resist Change, you chain yourself to the illusion of continuity. Break free. Acknowledge impermanence as your co-conspirator, not your foe. Instead of fossilizing plans, see them as fluid blueprints for reality yet to be sculpted. You're not losing; you're shedding, metamorphosing, evolving.

Give room to your sorrows, but don't let them build homes in you. Beauty is a passing landscape, as is suffering—a series of transitory brushstrokes on the grand canvas of existence.

And so, wake up to this impermanent symphony and make each cadence, each crescendo, and each silent pause truly yours. Abandon regret; it's a relic of a past self who didn't know better. Embrace the current moment as a radical act of rebellion against impermanence.

To live as if each moment is orchestrated in your favor—that, my friend, is the closest we come to touching eternity.

Journal Prompts

Answer each prompt with at least 2-3 paragraphs. Give yourself time and space to ask these questions, explore ideas, and use your imagination to answer.

Embracing Impermanence: Reflect on the concept of impermanence and its significance in Buddhism. How can embracing the idea that nothing is intended to last forever add value and beauty to your life? How can you cultivate a mindset that welcomes change and views it as an opportunity for growth?

Living in the Present: Consider the quote by Rumi, "Live life as if everything is rigged in your favor." How can adopting this perspective empower you to live fully in the present moment and let go of regrets or fears about the future? How can you find joy and purpose in each moment, despite the inevitable changes that life brings?

___
___
___
___
___
___
___
___
___
___
___
___
___
___
___
___
___
___

Exercise

Begin your exercise between 4-6 a.m.

Find your Awakening space.

Start in a standing position, and ground your bare feet into the Earth or floor beneath you.

When you're ready, practice the Awaken Breathwork Meditation.

LESSON SIX

The Path to Enlightenment

Objective:

To embrace the beauty of impermanence
and begin to live our lives to the fullest.

A Note of Love:
Your Path to Enlightenment

Enlightenment—less a destination, more an ever-unfolding tapestry. This path is not linear but fractal, tracing infinite patterns of awareness and consciousness. Your odyssey toward enlightenment is etched with paradoxes, fueled by the sublime and the mundane and elevated by authentic introspection.

Here, HUMILITY manifests not as self-deprecation but as an existential surrender, a yielding to the unfathomable grandeur of existence itself. In the shedding of illusionary veils, we find not absence but our untamed essence.

TRUTH, then, is your North Star in this labyrinthine journey. It doesn't pacify but agitates, urging you towards the unbalanced equilibrium where chaos and order commingle, perpetually inviting wholeness.

In the throes of CONNECTION, we're neither rootless wanderers nor static trees but the ever-expanding mycelium—our lives a complex web of relationships that feed our source power and amplify our existential resonance.

Through the lens of TRUST, the universe ceases to be a foreign expanse and transmutes into an intimate landscape. It is a symphony of synchronicities where each dissonant or harmonious note enriches the existential score.

GRATITUDE emerges not merely as an attitude but as a radical acceptance. It recognizes the intricate ballet of sorrow and joy, agony and ecstasy, as the fabric of our human tapestry.

ASPIRATION, then, is not about reaching an apex but spiraling inward and outward. The gyroscope navigates us through the liminal, eternally sculpting our cosmic self-portrait.

Within this unfathomable journey unfolds COMPASSION—a fierce tenderness that transcends sentimentality. It becomes a subversive act, an anarchic kindness that defies conditional metrics and enfolds us all in its boundless embrace.

So, let us be wayfarers on this enigmatic path.

And for your Morning Theta Meditation, consider:
"In the stillness of my heart, I touch eternity.
Present in the Now, I honor the sepia hues of yesterday.
Present in the Now, I untangle the nebulous threads of tomorrow.
Present in the Now, I become the artisan of my becoming."

Journal Prompts

Answer each prompt with at least 2-3 paragraphs. Give yourself time and space to ask these questions, explore ideas, and use your imagination to answer.

Humility: Have I made my life needlessly complex? If I have, what are the reasons behind it?

Truth: What truth do I need to give careful consideration to?

_____
_____
_____
_____
_____
_____
_____
_____
_____
_____
_____
_____
_____
_____
_____
_____
_____

Connection: What must be shed from the outer layers of my life so that my inner radiance can glow radiantly?

_____
_____
_____
_____
_____
_____
_____
_____
_____
_____
_____
_____
_____
_____
_____
_____

Trust: What should I release or embrace to strengthen my connection with faith?

_____

Gratitude: What am I waiting for? How can I break free from waiting and embrace a more fulfilling life going forward?

_____

Aspiration: How can I inspire the aspiration to embrace all the creation within and around me?

___

Compassion: How can I incorporate acts of loving-kindness into my daily life?

___

AWAKEN
CLOSING PRAYER

Dear Universe, Divine Source, and all that is sacred,

As we gather here at the culmination of our Awaken journey, we offer gratitude for the wisdom and insight gained. We acknowledge the divine presence that guided us through these transformative moments.

We thank you for the clarity and self-discovery we've found within the embrace of each breath. We recognize the light within us, reflecting your eternal wisdom and grace.

As we close this chapter, we ask for your continued guidance and blessings on our paths. May the lessons we've learned during our time together continue to illuminate our way forward.

Grant us the strength to carry the mindfulness and self-belief we've cultivated into the world. May we use these gifts to create positive change in our lives and th those we touch.ose we touch.

We release any doubts or fears that hold us back and embrace the courage to step into the next phase of our journey. May we carry the lessons of this Awaken stage with us as we navigate the world's challenges and joys.

In your infinite wisdom, help us to turn the page with grace, knowing that we are forever connected to the wisdom within us and the guidance of the cosmos.

Thank you for this time of self-discovery, growth, and transformation. May we walk this path with open hearts and minds, ready to embrace the new beginnings that await.

With Loving Intentions, My Body, My Mind, My Spirit.

We are now entering the last stage of grief, Eat Healthy, Warriors,

Journeys can take straightforward routes, while others meander through uncertainty. Sometimes, people come together to lend support and lighten the burden. Regardless of the challenges we face on our journeys, there's an opportunity to reach a particular destination—a place where our innermost desires align with our soul's longing—where we find a radiant glow of unconditional love.

Let us acknowledge and honor the paths we've traversed and those that lie ahead as we awaken to the present moment.

With Purposeful Intentions,

MiMi

Please explore my jewelry collection. The UNALOME symbolizes the path toward enlightenment, and each piece is designed as a reminder of the inner strength and courage we all possess.
Visit www.StoryOf11.com to discover these meaningful creations.

CONNECT
The Sixth Stage of Grief

EMBRACE

MICHELE C. BELL
THE GRIEF WARRIOR®

you've made it

You are now ready to EMBRACE our Sixth Stage:

— connect —

That's the blessing and power of **pivoting with purpose.**

What are the 7 Stages of Grief Alignment?
Express. **M**editate.
Be Present. **R**ejuvenate.
Awaken. **C**onnect. **E**at Healthy.

Healing begins with acceptance and alignment transforms us through embracing our circumstances.

The empower of embracing is in your next chapter – are you ready to turn the page?

WELCOME
let's reconnect

Grand Rising, Warriors!

It's The Grief Warrior® — your guide, mentor, and companion on your journey to EMBRACE.

I know you're still healing. Maybe you don't feel like you've even started healing yet.
Wherever you are on your journey, you are welcome here.

Grief has the power to both connect and disconnect us from what we love. Even when surrounded by support and opportunity, we feel alone.

Like nobody understands. Like we'll never be the same.

And the truth is, we won't be the same. Life is a continual shitshow of change, heartache, and chaos. But that's also the beautiful part of it.

We're wired to grow, learn, and evolve every day. When we resist this change, we disconnect who we are and who we can become.

So, take my hand. Together, we'll connect our pasts, presents, and futures. We'll move WITH our grief, embracing what is and is to come.

Let's reconnect with our lives. Our loved ones. And most importantly, ourselves."

**Thank you for embracing your true self.
You've earned this moment.**

Table of Contents

Welcome 03

Lesson 1: Let Go To Let Yourself Glow 06

Lesson 2: Bridging the Gap Between You & Your Inner Child 10

Lesson 3: Find Wisdom in Every Day 18

Lesson 4: Reborn to Reconnect 24

Lesson 5: Unbury Your Pain to Uncover Your Purpose 29

Lesson 6: Follow Your Path 35

Unveiling the Threads of Connection: Guided Mantra for Spiritual Insight

After completing every chapter, we will establish a sacred rite of interconnection. Embrace these instructions as a sacred scroll, guiding you toward harmony in the pursuit of aligning oneself with the intricate dance of body, mind, and spirit; it is wise to dedicate a mere twenty minutes to each exercise.

Repeat this mantra:
"In the tranquil embrace of my heart, I unearth the profound serenity within me. In embracing the present moment, I pay homage to the cherished memories of yesteryear. In embracing the present moment, I release the burdens of tomorrow's anxieties. By embracing the essence of the present moment, I possess the power to mold the very fabric of my existence."

Enlightenment is the profound odyssey of harmonizing with the depths of your inner wisdom, forging a sacred bond with the whispers of your inner compass, the reservoir of knowledge and benevolence that transcends the superficial veneer of existence. It grants you the profound ability to perceive the world in its unadulterated essence, unveiling the veils that shroud your genuine being. The journey toward enlightenment is adorned with contemplation, profound introspection, and ethereal encounters, where one embraces each passing moment and assimilates the teachings of life in unison.

The Art of Spiritual Connection
SPIRIT Walk

Introducing the 7 tools of contemplation, reflection, and mystical experience will deepen this meaningful connection to self.

In our quest for **CONNECTION**, we open our hearts to receive -- deepening our roots, nurturing our growth, and harmonizing our existence, honoring our truth.

On this sacred journey, we are exploring the concept of **HUMILITY**, letting go of idealism and attachment to embrace the essence of our most authentic selves.

Like a luminous aura, **ASPIRATION** beckons us to contemplate our inner realm and the splendor that envelops us.

The quest for **TRUST** becomes our most loyal ally, illuminating our path and guiding us toward the sacred equilibrium.

Inviting **TRUTH** into our landscape, its power enables us to open our awareness to the spiritual truth within our inner sanctuary.

In the pursuit of **GRATITUDE**, we immerse ourselves in the opulence of our human journey and nurture a profound sense of appreciation within our souls.

In this profound odyssey, we encounter the essence of **COMPASSION**, embracing the art of boundless tenderness towards both our souls and the souls of others.

"Every journey we embark upon is unique—some straightforward, others meandering, some filled with bravery, and others riddled with uncertainty. Yet, every journey, when pursued with honesty and sincerity, holds the potential to lead us to a destination where our profound joy aligns with the world's profound purpose."

Be still and relearn to love you.

LESSON 1

Let Go to Let Yourself Glow

OBJECTIVE:
To release what's no longer serving us to make more room for what will.

A NOTE OF LOVE:
Give Yourself Space to Heal

We have both heard it too many times.

"It's time to move on. Get over it."

But you and I both know that's not how it works.

Moving on isn't embracing. Moving on is resisting what's in front of you. No — we must connect with our pain. Sit with it for a quiet moment. Make room for ourselves to heal so we can move WITH our grief.

But to make room for our healing, we must make space, starting with the other pains from our pasts that we have carried for far too long.

Whether in this life — or past lives — you've collected much cargo. Now, we're here to unpack this baggage and ask:
"Is this truly mine to carry?"

Your fears. Your limiting beliefs. Your bad habits.

Do these beliefs originate from you, or have they been inherited from your ancestors, friends, society, or the media? It's important to consider if someone else's unresolved trauma influences them.

Ask yourself what's not yours to carry — and release it. It's in letting go of what no longer serves us that we make more room for what does.

As you *move with*, you have more room to grow. You can move with your fear, pain, and memories. You already have for so long.

But some aren't yours to carry any longer. Allow yourself to pause - observe...

Be present. Look within. And allow yourself to release what is no longer — and never was — yours.

JOURNAL PROMPTS

Answer each prompt with at least 1-3 paragraphs. Give yourself time to reflect, connect, and sit with your answers.

Letting Go of Fear

What are some things that cause fear within me?

_____
_____
_____
_____

What is the origin of these fears?

_____
_____
_____
_____

Are these fears belong to me or were they inherited from someone else?

_____
_____
_____
_____

How can I rewrite this fear to serve my personal growth and progress?

_____
_____
_____
_____

JOURNAL PROMPTS

Letting Go of Limiting Beliefs

Reflect on the notion of "moving on" versus "embracing." How do these two concepts differ in your understanding of grief and healing? How might embracing your pain and sitting with it, rather than resisting it, impact your healing journey?

_____
_____
_____
_____

Take a moment to examine the baggage you've been carrying from your past. What fears, limiting beliefs, or bad habits do you recognize as potential burdens you may have inherited from others? How might releasing these burdens create more space for healing and growth?

_____
_____
_____
_____

Explore the idea of inherited trauma and its influence on your beliefs and emotions. Are there aspects of your pain that may not originate from your personal experiences but could be passed down from previous generations or societal influences? How might understanding this concept help you navigate your healing process more compassionately?

_____
_____
_____
_____

Consider the liberating power of releasing what is not truly yours to carry. What emotions or memories might you hold that no longer serve your growth and well-being? How can you create a safe and nurturing space to release these burdens and make room for a more authentic and expansive self?

_____
_____
_____
_____

EXERCISE

Let's start with your first Connectivity Practice. Take 20 minutes to connect with your mind, body, and spirit. Find your space—the root of a tree - sitting in nature.

- Start a timer and take a moment to appreciate the beauty in your surroundings. Whether you meditate, journal, or walk in nature, make a mental note of what you are grateful for and what you find beautiful.

- Embrace the tranquility and take on the task of pondering over things that evoke feelings of connection and inspiration.

> Yesterday was heavy. Release them. The tale of tomorrow is yet unwritten. Let it be. Allow it to unfold. Today belongs to you. Embrace it moment by moment. Connect your presence, make today your own, and dwell in the present.
>
> In the coming moments, seek your tranquility in the gentle rhythm of your breathing. Seek gratitude and the beauty around you. PAUSE. OBSERVE: Engaging in a period of meditation, jotting down personal reflections in a journal, or taking a leisurely walk in nature can all serve as valuable ways to reflect and gain clarity.
>
> Caring for, loving, and healing what we feel estranged is difficult. We're here to rekindle this bond with yourself, so you can manage, love, and heal yourself again.
>
> **Be still and relearn to love you.**

LESSON 2

Bridging the Gap Between You & Your Inner Child

OBJECTIVE:
To nurture your inner child, break free from your self-sabotaging patterns, and connect with your childlike joy.

A NOTE OF LOVE:
Reconnect. Reignite. Reparent.

Recall your youth. Imagine everything about your past self.

Do you think these instances feel like distant memories? Do they seem like faded, vintage photos or characters from a story of your past?

Your inner child always remains with you, but occasionally, we tend to move on without them.

Our inner child is the embodiment of naivety and fragility. Their presence is evident in our fears, choices, relationships, and sorrows. They sparkle through our inquisitiveness, inventiveness, and joy.

However, when our early years were shadowed with more suffering than joy, we often wished to leave them behind.

In doing so, the fragile feelings of desertion and solitude intensify.

Your inner child can undermine you. Not necessarily intentionally, but as a cry for acknowledgment. A plea for healing. A call for re-parenting.

Engaging in self-reparenting is essential to strengthen our connection with our inner child. There comes a time when we need to reconcile with ourselves and offer the stability, courage, and love we yearned for in those early years.

A NOTE OF LOVE:
Reconnect. Reignite. Reparent.

Reflect on the feelings you harbored as a young one—your inner child is still wrestling with these emotions.

What self-destructive behaviors do you find yourself caught up in? What recurring patterns trap you?

Often these patterns are all too familiar, but they remain fragments and remnants of our history.

As you navigate these emotions, you can extend your hand, connect and gain control of the steering wheel.

So, spend some time with little you.

Indulge in messiness. Let laughter, chirps, and playful moments envelop you.

Revisit your childhood favorite books, indulge in your most special shows, and let your curiosity and creativity run wild.

Embrace painting by numbers or coloring beyond boundaries. Peruse old pictures, and send grace to that innocent, mischievous smile.

Let your guard down, and let your inner child gleam without criticism.

Then, when you both feel secure in each other's company, you can clasp hands and progress together.

Offer yourself empathy. Break the cycle, and be present for them. Forge a bond with your inner child, and they'll unveil a new realm for you.

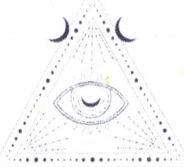

JOURNAL PROMPTS

*Step 1: Write a letter to your inner child. Give them the grace, compassion, and healing they deserve. Use these prompts to help guide your letter:

Write a Letter to Your Inner Child

What fears did I have during my childhood?

_____
_____
_____
_____

As a child, which emotions did I feel most often?

_____
_____
_____
_____

When I was a child, what were the things that made me happy, calm, and loved?

_____
_____
_____
_____

As a child, what were the words that I needed to hear?

_____
_____
_____
_____

 # JOURNAL PROMPTS

Reflection on the Past: Write about a specific memory from your childhood that stands out, whether joyful or painful. How does this memory impact your feelings and decisions today? Is it a memory your inner child holds onto tightly?

_____
_____
_____
_____

Letter to Your Younger Self: If you were to write a letter to yourself at age 10, what would you say? What advice or comfort would you offer? What praises would you share?

_____
_____
_____
_____

Feelings of Abandonment: Recall a time when you felt particularly abandoned or isolated in your younger years. How has that shaped your relationships and coping mechanisms today?

_____
_____
_____
_____

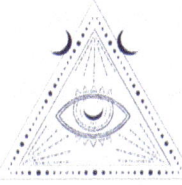

JOURNAL PROMPTS

*Step 2: Write a response letter from your inner child. Imagine what they have to say after receiving your first letter.

Give your present self the grace, compassion, and healing you gave your inner child. Use these prompts to help guide your response letter:

Write a Letter From Your Inner Child

Inner Child's Voice: Write a dialogue between your current self and your inner child. What are the fears, hopes, and dreams your inner child would voice out? How would you, as an adult, respond?

___
___
___

Visions of Childhood: Visualize a photograph from your past that captures a significant moment. Describe the photo in detail. What emotions are present? How does this frozen moment in time resonate with you now?

___
___
___

Steps to Re-parenting: List three specific ways you can self-reparenting to heal and reconnect with your inner child. How can you provide the stability, courage, and love you needed back then?

___
___
___

A Healing Moment: Think of a time when you acknowledged and cared for your inner child in a significant way. How did that make you feel? If you have not had such an experience, envision a situation where you could.

___
___
___

JOURNAL PROMPTS

What soothing phrases or affirmations can I offer to heal and reassure my inner child?
___
___
___
___

How can the insights from my younger self-guide and enrich my journey ahead?
___
___
___
___

How can I nurture and express love to the child within me and the person I am today?
___
___
___
___

INNER CHILD VISION BOARD EXERCISE

Purpose: To visually represent your connection with your inner child, understand past emotions, and visualize the healing and nurturing you want to provide.

Materials:
- A large piece of poster board or cardboard
- Old magazines, newspapers, photos, or printouts
- Scissors
- Glue or tape
- Markers, colored pencils, or paints

Steps:
1. **Preparation:** Clear a workspace and gather all your materials. Ensure you have a comfortable, calm environment to work in.
2. **Reflect:** Take a moment to remember your childhood and jot down any memories, emotions, or wants that come to mind.
3. **Search for Images:** Look for pictures that match your thoughts about your inner child in magazines or newspapers. They can represent memories, emotions, aspirations, or current desires.
4. **Cut and Sort:** As you find relevant images or words, cut them out. Group them loosely based on themes or feelings they evoke.
5. **Layout:** Before gluing anything, arrange your images on your board. Consider placing:
    - Memories or feelings on the left side.
    - Present feelings or acknowledgments in the center.
    - Future hopes, self-reparenting goals, and reconciliation on the right side.
6. **Embellish with Words or Drawings:** Use markers, colored pencils, or paints to add thoughts, dreams, or affirmations. For instance, you might write "It's okay to feel" or "I am here for you now" to emphasize the message of self-reparenting.
7. **Glue Everything Down**: Once you're satisfied with the layout, start gluing or taping down your images and words.
8. **Reflection:** Once your board is complete, take a step back. What feelings emerge as you look at the board? Consider writing a brief reflection or letter to your inner child based on the visuals you've chosen.
9. **Display:** Place your vision board somewhere you'll see it regularly. It's a visual reminder of your commitment to nurturing and reconciling with your inner child.
10. **Regular Check-ins:** Every few weeks or months, take a moment to sit with your vision board. Reflect on your progress in your self-reparenting journey and any new feelings or realizations that have emerged.

This vision board serves as a creative outlet and a tangible reminder of the importance of recognizing, understanding, and caring for your inner child.

LESSON 3

Find Wisdom in Every Day

OBJECTIVE:
Discover life's lessons by being mindful
of the wisdom and teachings
surrounding you.

A NOTE OF LOVE:
Uncovering Your Life Lessons

Life is our teacher. She's a challenging yet gentle one — she discerns when to reprimand when to reward, and when to let us navigate independently.

The problem is that we're not always the best students. We often stop heeding her lessons, assuming we know best, despite the stark truths before us.

However, once we acknowledge that we are simply learners in the grand classroom of life, we relieve the pressure of perfection. We can sometimes be 'right.' Everything around us doesn't need to be 'right' — our role is to learn from it.

If life speaks to us, our task is to pay attention. This perspective ignites our dormant childlike curiosity, bridging the gap to our inner child. We can explore freely if the world is our learning ground and playground.

Isn't it liberating to realize we don't hold the reins to everything?

Regardless of their scale, life imparts lessons daily. We must attune to them and allow them to steer us to our destined place, where we are meant to be.

Frequently, these lessons are unveiled in pain, sorrow, trauma, and tribulations. Even in monotony, stagnation, and solitude, we can unearth wisdom.

But we can only access this wisdom if we CONNECT.

We must connect to life as our teachers by EMBRACING the PRESENT and regarding our encounters and experiences as nuggets of wisdom, fostering growth, and illuminating truths.

A NOTE OF LOVE:
Uncovering Your Life Lessons

Become a wise observer and active participant in your life. Remember: You're the main character of your story, yet a background character for another. Find perspective in this. Seek to understand the stories around you, like a child enveloped in their new favorite book. Stop chasing what you need to learn and start embracing and accepting what's already around you.

Connect with yourself. Find the lessons already within you, waiting to rise to the surface. Get to know yourself in your actual, authentic state. Take time to get to know yourself and become aware of your life, mind, body, and soul.

This is where you connect with your life lessons. This is where you connect with your life's purpose.

Without learning, pain is simply pain. Without grace, grief is merely grief. We can thank human nature for our ability to create meaning, uncover stories, and build connections that turn pain into purpose and empower grace in our grief.

As a healing practitioner, I help my clients navigate the path to wisdom with a physical journey to an inspired destination. As we explore new territories, we map life lessons and pave the way to new destinations. This path to uncovering our purposes and unlocking our lessons often requires another guide.

Wherever you are, open yourself up to a new journey—a new destination. Leap and make a move. Show the universe and yourself that you're ready to receive wisdom. That you're prepared to learn, listen, and love.

Life is ready to connect you to your purpose. Will you receive it?

JOURNAL PROMPTS

Answer each prompt with at least 1-3 paragraphs. Give yourself time to reflect, connect, and sit with your answers.

Find Wisdom in Every Day

In what moments have I felt most connected to life's lessons, and how did those moments shape my perspective on growth and purpose?

_____
_____
_____
_____

Recall when pain, sorrow, or a challenging situation unveiled a profound lesson. How can I reframe similar experiences in the future to extract wisdom from them?

_____
_____
_____
_____

How can I deepen my connection with myself to understand better the stories and lessons that are waiting to emerge from within?

_____
_____
_____
_____

JOURNAL PROMPTS

Find Wisdom Today

When was the last time I fully embraced the present moment, seeking its hidden lessons and wisdom? How can I practice this mindfulness more frequently?

_____
_____
_____
_____

How does the concept of being both the main character in my story and a background character in someone else's impact my understanding of relationships and my role in the world?

_____
_____
_____
_____

Think about a time when life tried to teach you something but you resisted the lesson. In hindsight, what wisdom was life offering, and how can you open your heart to receive such teachings more gracefully in the future?

_____
_____
_____
_____

EXERCISE

Begin your next Connectivity Practice. Take 20 minutes to connect with your mind, body, and spirit.

- Set a timer and begin to look for the surrounding beauty. Note what you're grateful for and what you find beautiful as you meditate, journal, or walk in nature.

- You may approach this exercise with a curiosity to learn, the patience to pause and listen, or the willingness to receive wisdom.

LESSON 4

Reborn to Reconnect

OBJECTIVE:
To make peace with the present,
reconnect to this moment, and allow
yourself to Pause.

A NOTE OF LOVE:
The Power of The Pause

You're familiar with these age-old expressions:

"As one narrative concludes, another unfolds." "When one portal shuts, another opens."

We frequently perceive life as a ceaseless accumulation of objects, memories, and accomplishments. We devote days, months, or even years desiring and striving for our ambitions, only to immediately replace them with fresh ones. As soon as we cross off an item on our agenda, we hastily add a new one.

We run from life transitions. We fear being trapped in the "limbo," the waiting rooms of life — the periods where we're waiting to heal, for our opportunity, and for things to feel "normal" again.

But what if the healing, opportunity, and "normal" you're looking for are found in your life's waiting rooms? What if your reconnection lies BETWEEN your life's chapters and doorways?

This is what I like to call the power of The Pause.

The most profound way to heal is to engage with The Pause. You don't need to resolve all your issues or complete your list of tasks. There's no need for haste, no need to work tirelessly. Take your time thinking. Don't pass judgment. Pause.

Listen to your voice. Discover tranquility despite the upheaval. Allow yourself to adjust to this state of "limbo."

Ultimately, your happiness isn't contingent upon moving from Point A to Point B. We live most of our lives in these transitional zones. Thus, we reconnect with ourselves by uncovering serenity, strength, and meaning within these stages.

By allowing ourselves to Pause for long enough, we rediscover our purpose, vitality, and awareness.

Of course, this is more challenging in practice than in theory. Often, when we feel trapped in our life's waiting rooms, we've likely just emerged from our darkest chapters. We yearn to turn back time. We long to fast-forward.

A NOTE OF LOVE:
The Power of The Pause

We yearn to do anything but remain in this present moment of anticipation. Let's not deceive ourselves - it's a bitter pill to swallow. Our existence irrevocably alters when we suffer the loss of a person or an entity that holds significant meaning in our lives.

From this void arises the intersection of the "limbo" — unable to revert or leap ahead, things can seem gloomy.

We feel isolated. Perplexed. Disoriented. Truthfully, it's unsettling.

And it's precisely within these confines that we have two choices: to either sink further into the abyss or chart our course towards personal growth.

We shift our energy when we embrace the Pause and find a presence in this pain.

We realize that we've endured and blossomed through numerous transformations and transitions. We've lost so much and gained so much. We've greeted many new beginnings and bid farewell to various endings. We've adapted and progressed amidst daily changes.

And in these infinite shifts, we must seek The Pause. We need to move in harmony with our pain, not resist it.

Like sunflowers, we gradually ascend, grow, and turn toward the sunlight. Connecting to this moment, we pave the way for recovery. While it's slow and often invisible to the human eye, a gradual and ongoing process occurs.

Pause for yourself. Pause for the pain of others. Give yourself space to connect. This is our sanctuary for healing. This is where we reconnect. This is our place of rebirth.

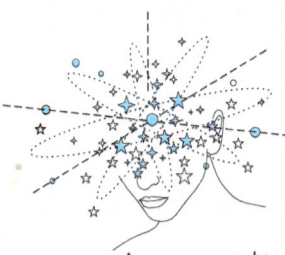

JOURNAL PROMPTS

Answer each prompt with at least 1-3 paragraphs. Give yourself time to reflect, connect, and sit with your answers.

The Power of The Pause

Reflect on a significant transition in your life. How did you initially react, and what did you discover during "The Pause" in that waiting room of life?

_____
_____
_____
_____

When you feel the urge to rush through a challenging moment, what are some strategies or reminders you can use to anchor yourself in the power of The Pause?

_____
_____
_____
_____

Think of a time when you resisted "limbo" or felt impatient with life's waiting room. How did that resistance serve or hinder your growth?

_____
_____
_____
_____

What rituals or practices can you cultivate to find solace and reconnect with your purpose during life's transitional zones?

_____
_____
_____
_____

# EXERCISE

Start your next connectivity practice by taking 20 minutes to connect with your mind, body, and spirit.

- Set a timer and begin to look for the beauty around you. Note what you're grateful for and what you find beautiful as you meditate, journal, or walk in nature.

- In envisioning the impact you wish to have on the world, what meaningful endeavors or causes align with your purpose and can be pursued during this period of reflection?

- How can you ensure that your purpose during The Pause extends beyond this temporary break and becomes integral to your ongoing journey towards a more purposeful and fulfilling life?

- You may approach this exercise with a curiosity to learn, the patience to pause and listen, or the willingness to receive wisdom.

LESSON 5

Unbury Your Pain to Uncover Your Purpose

OBJECTIVE:
To explore our pains, heal our pasts,
and create a deep-rooted purpose.

A NOTE OF LOVE:
No More Pushing

We've been conditioned to suppress our feelings from childhood when distressing events occur.

Society categorized emotions as "positive" and "negative." We received praise for our laughter but were often discouraged when we displayed anger, sorrow, or vexation.

We were socialized to bury our suffering, to "maintain a cheerful exterior," and persist regardless. We're choosing not to take care of it right now... we'll manage it later.

We've become so proficient at concealing our distress that we occasionally lose sight of it until we suddenly can't.

Until one day, the pain resurfaces. We face a loss. Our past trauma revisits us. We endure the unfiltered pain of being human. We attempt to use the defenses of our younger selves, trying to bury, cover-up, and disguise our suffering. But as we suppress these emotions, they start to overwhelm us. As the saying goes, "It's the last straw that breaks the camel's back."

Burying our emotions only leaves them unresolved. They can fester, evolve, and warp how we experience the world. They can form blocks in our minds, bodies, and even spirits, creating physical manifestations of our trauma.

But in unburying them, we can begin to heal. We need to reconnect with our emotions, histories, and recollections to permit ourselves to evolve. Life is a cyclical journey. The past is not just "behind us." We don't simply "get over it."

Our existence is a continuous connection and progression from this precise instant. To fully engage with and EMBRACE the present, we must unpack our past and future.

When we hide from our pain, it doesn't disappear. It stays, feeling unhealed, unloved, and neglected. By burying our pain, we imply that our healing is unimportant when nothing could be more crucial.

But when we unbury, unpack, and unravel our pain, we can begin to understand our lives, ourselves, and our pasts. In this space, we can gain insight into our futures.

A NOTE OF LOVE:
No More Pushing

To feel pain is to find your reason for being. Every hero and legendary figure in mythology has a tragic history. They discovered what they were here to do after suffering loss, tragedy, or anguish.

Pain can guide us toward helping others through shared experiences. For me, it was the experience of grief and loss. As I grappled with an unthinkable loss, I sought out others in similar situations.

I thought, "We shouldn't have to navigate this alone." Today, I give others the same support, guidance, and resilience I wish I could give myself years ago.

How can you transmute your pain into a gentle, illuminated path for others to embrace?

What experiences are distinctively yours? What hardships have shaped, formed, and determined who you are today?

Embrace this. Engage with it. Allow yourself room to be present with your chaos. You don't need to hide it. You can be simultaneously battling and resilient. Disorganized and driven. You are grieving yet growing.

No more pushing. No more pushing away your emotions, your pain, or your past. We restrain ourselves through resistance but glow through acceptance, surrender, and embrace.

As you unbury your pain, you also unearth your purpose. It's time to connect with it.

JOURNAL PROMPTS

Answer each prompt with at least 1-3 paragraphs. Give yourself time to reflect, connect, and sit with your answers.

Unbury Your Pain to Uncover Your Purpose

Reflect on when you were encouraged to suppress a "negative" emotion. How did it shape your understanding of that emotion, and how do you approach it now?

_____
_____
_____
_____

Recall a painful or traumatic event from your past. How has this experience influenced your current outlook, behaviors, or relationships? How can you use this understanding to guide others or grow personally?

_____
_____
_____
_____

What emotions or memories have you buried deep within, and what triggers or events bring them to the surface? How can you begin to address and embrace these feelings healthily?

_____
_____
_____
_____

 # JOURNAL PROMPTS

Answer each prompt with at least 1-3 paragraphs. Give yourself time to reflect, connect, and sit with your answers.

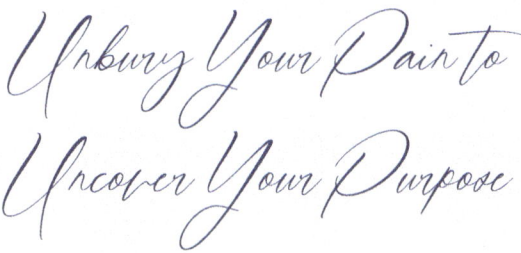

Unbury Your Pain to Uncover Your Purpose

Consider a time when your buried emotions manifested in unexpected ways – physically, mentally, or spiritually. How did you recognize the connection, and what steps did you take (or can take) to heal and integrate those feelings?

_____
_____
_____
_____

If your buried emotions could speak, what would they say? Envision a future where these emotions are channeled into purpose and passion. How can I view this impact from a place of purpose and grace?

_____
_____
_____
_____

EXERCISE

"Facing our pain uncovers our true purpose; it's not a burden, but a beacon leading us to our authentic path."

Begin your next Connectivity Practice. Take 20 minutes to connect with your mind, body, and spirit.

- Set a timer and begin to look for the surrounding beauty. Note what you're grateful for and what you find beautiful as you meditate, journal, or walk in nature.
- How do you see your experiences of pain influencing your unique path to discover your purpose?
- How might you turn uncovering your pain into a transformative journey toward realizing your purpose?
- Allow yourself to feel any emotions that come up. Don't resist any thoughts, feelings, or sensations. Accept, surrender, and embrace. Let it flow. You don't have to hide anymore.

LESSON 6

Follow Your Path

OBJECTIVE:
Trust in ourselves, make peace with the present and strengthen our connection with intuition and wisdom.

A NOTE OF LOVE:
You Have the Answers — Listen.

It can be scary when we allow ourselves to feel again. Overwhelming. Uncomfortable.

As we shed layers of security and accept the rawness of healing, we start to evolve and seek resolution. People may try to dictate the "proper" way to heal, grieve, or progress while you search for answers.

But only you know this answer.

You are connected to the Universe, your Higher Power, and your Source of Energy. When you tune into this connection, you replace fear with faith.

You find courage and confidence, even in uncertainty about the future! Remember – the insights you're seeking are already embedded within your inner sanctuary.

Embrace the trust that the Universe is your steadfast ally, and equally, have faith that you are your reliable companion. In this realm of faith, you can pivot from pain to a journey of purpose. You can transform by acknowledging the full strength and wisdom in your being.

When we contemplate "following our path," we often envision a grand, dramatic unveiling — a concealed purpose that will suddenly appear miraculously ready to metamorphose our lives one day.

But our purposes are already present within us. The answers you seek lie within your spirit. You have the inner compass. You carry an internal compass. You won't discover your healing trajectory by comparing it with others. Introspection will reveal it by taking a pause. Reflecting. Breathing. Your path will illuminate before you by simply existing in the present moment.

A NOTE OF LOVE:
You Have the Answers — Listen.

Ignite this bond with your inner self, and you'll unveil the wisdom within you.

Bear in mind: This is The Pause: each day, serene moments are utilized for reflection, connection, and achieving lucidity.

In these moments, we let go of the need to control, skip to the book's last page, and fast-forward to the end. That's not where the answers are. The answers you're looking for are in between the pages and paragraphs. They're in the very life chapter you're currently navigating.

Just because someone else is on a different chapter doesn't mean you're behind — you're merely experiencing other narratives.

Your decisions. Remember: You are the author. While you may not always be able to forecast every aspect of your narrative, you hold the reins to your destiny.

There's no universally "correct" way to mourn. There's no set schedule for healing. The journey manifests differently for each one of us.

Your journey through grief is uniquely yours. You will discover your path when it's the right moment for you. Trust the process, and have faith in yourself.

You have everything you need to heal.

Align with the power already present within you. Be patient.

Remember The Pause. The solutions aren't found in rushing forward but in breathing and existing here, in the present moment.

JOURNAL PROMPTS

Answer each prompt with at least 1-3 paragraphs. Give yourself time to reflect, connect, and sit with your answers.

Follow Your Path

The Pause Reflection: Consider a recent situation where you must rush to a conclusion. How might you have benefited from embracing "The Pause" instead?

_____
_____
_____
_____

Author of Your Narrative: What would the current chapter be titled if your life was a book? Describe the key events and emotions in this chapter.

_____
_____
_____
_____

In-Between Moments: Recollect a seemingly insignificant moment from the past week — something between the 'big events.' What wisdom or realization can you derive from this often-overlooked experience?

_____
_____
_____
_____

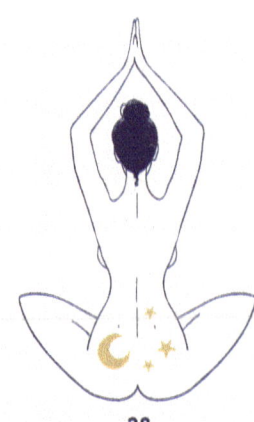

JOURNAL PROMPTS

Answer each prompt with at least 1-3 paragraphs. Give yourself time to reflect, connect, and sit with your answers.

Follow Your Path

Comparative Journey: Reflect on a time when you felt behind because others seemed ahead in their life's journey. How can you shift your perspective to understand that your unique narrative is neither behind nor ahead, but just right for you?

_____
_____
_____
_____

Healing Timeline: Write about a past wound or trauma. How has your healing process for this experience been unique? Are there any pressures you feel from external sources on how you should heal, and how can you let go of these to honor your journey?

_____
_____
_____
_____

Power Within: Identify a strength or quality within yourself that you often overlook. How can this internal power aid in your healing and personal growth? Remember to align with this power during moments of self-doubt.

_____
_____
_____
_____

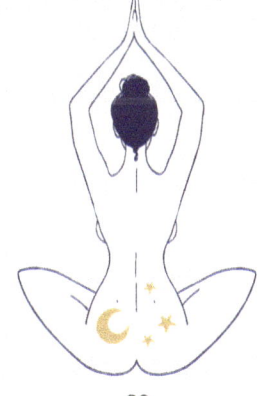

EXERCISE

Begin your next Connectivity Practice: Use the prompts blow to begin.

- Set a timer (30 mins each exercise) Note what you're grateful for and what you find beautiful as you meditate, journal, or walk in nature.

- Trust yourself as you reflect and connect. Let your thoughts and intuition lead, trusting that you'll be led to growth, hope, and healing.

Mind-Body-Spirit Vision Board

Craft a vision board that visually represents your path, not just in material or external achievements but feelings, growth, and spiritual aspirations.

Divide the board into three sections: Mind, Body, and Spirit. For the Mind, include images or words representing your intellectual growth, learning goals, or creativity. For the Body, display representations of health, wellness, vitality, or physical challenges you wish to undertake. Lastly, for the Spirit, choose images or phrases that reflect your inner values, spiritual growth, or a sense of purpose.

This creative exercise solidifies your path visually and serves as a daily reminder to stay aligned and connected with your mind, body, and spirit.

Journey Meditation

This exercise invites you on a meditative journey to connect with your path deeply.

Start by finding a comfortable, quiet place to sit or stand with a relaxed posture. Take a moment to breathe, allowing each breath to ground you in the present.
Now, gaze softly at these words and let them guide you. Imagine yourself at the beginning of a path. This path is a representation of your life journey. As you mentally tread this path, engage your senses. What might you see on this journey? Can you hear the subtle sounds around you? Feel the essence of this path and its significance in your heart. As you move along in your mind's eye, allow events or experiences from your journey to come forth. Don't judge or analyze them; acknowledge them.

Engaging with this exercise can offer profound insights about your current path, helping you align your mind, body, and spirit. As you finish, take a deep breath and let the feeling of connection linger in your journal. Whenever you're ready, continue with your day, carrying the insights and tranquility from this meditation.

Continue, Not Conclusion

Dear Courageous Warriors,

As the sun sets on our shared voyage in the CONNECT stage, it is a gentle transition, not an end. Much like a tale in a series of chronicles, our adventure prepares us for the next chapter.

As we journey through the 7 Stages of Grief, a powerful urge may arise within many of us, a longing to rewrite our stories swiftly.
Yet, I'd like to remind you of the ancient trees and persistent blooms. Their tale is told not in sudden leaps but in quiet, steadfast growth.

PAUSE. BEHOLD. PONDER.

As we step into tomorrow, I beckon you to join me in embracing our forthcoming chapter: Nourishing with Eating Healthy. In tending to the vessel that houses our spirit, we begin the alchemy of mending the soul. In cherishing ourselves, we praise our inner sanctum's worth.

For, in the end, what is truer than the act of self-love?

With Intention & Affection,

MiMi®

EAT HEALTHY
The Seventh Stage of Grief

EMBRACE

MICHELE C. BELL
THE GRIEF WARRIOR®

you've made it

You are now ready to **EAT HEALTHY in** our Final Stage:

eat healthy

That's the blessing and power of **pivoting with purpose.**

What are the 7 Stages of Grief Alignment?
Express. **M**editate.
Be Present. **R**ejuvenate.
Awaken. **C**onnect. **E**at Healthy.

The power of embracing awaits as you stand at the cusp of this last stage of our journey chapters.

**The question remains:
Are you prepared to journey onward and upward?**

Table of Contents

Lesson 1: Gut Health 101 05
Lesson 2: Ayurveda 11
Lesson 3: Find the Right Diet for You 21
Lesson 4: The Spiritual Cleanse of Fasting 28
Lesson 5: Mindful Eating 36
Lesson 6: Embrace Forward 42
Bath Recipes 50

WELCOME
Tuning into Your Body

Grand Rising, Wellness Warriors!

This final pillar of EMBRACE —
emphasizes the importance of
EATING HEALTHY

As we arrive at this pivotal moment in our EMBRACE journey, let's acknowledge the profound essence of EATING HEALTHY.

This final stride towards embracing our holistic selves is about taking decisive mental and physical steps. It's about harnessing the wisdom and strength we've accumulated thus far and putting it into daily practice. When we embrace compassion and adopt fresh perspectives, we fortify our mind, body, and spirit, enabling us to live with purpose and intention based on the insights we've garnered throughout our journey.

Treating our bodies respectfully isn't just a choice; it's a testament to understanding their value. Think of your body as a cherished home, a sacred space that requires care and attention. When we choose foods rich in nutrients, we cater to our physical well-being and sharpen our mental clarity.

As we delve deeper into EMBRACE, we must remain present and attentive. We've all been guilty of eating without truly appreciating the flavors, textures, and nourishment that our food provides. However, this guide aims to change that. Through its pages, we'll uncover the transformative power of mindful eating, turning our daily meals into moments of self-healing and gratitude.

By the end, we hope to instill an enduring appreciation for food as a source of nourishment and well-being.

I hope you enjoy every page, every word, and every taste.

With Infinite Intention,

The Grief Warrior

Sacred Cleanse

It is recommended to flush once a month, ideally during a full moon.

1 Quart of Distilled Water
1 Teaspoon of Aluminum Free Baking Soda
1 Teaspoon of Sea Salt

Start this cleanse in the morning.
Mix until thoroughly mixed.
Divide into four doses in a glass.
Drink every two hours.

With Infinite Intention,

The Grief Warrior

*Suggested recommendations can be purchased on my website
*Please read the recipe disclosure before starting any kind of cleanse

LESSON 1

Gut Health 101: Education Begins at the Kitchen Table

OBJECTIVE:
To explore the gut-brain connection and create a healing inner sanctuary.

A NOTE OF LOVE

Trust Your Gut

Shall we discuss food?

Food serves a purpose beyond sustaining our existence. Our mealtimes dictate our social events, internal routines, and daily schedules.

But what we eat is even more central than this.

Our bodies serve as our instruments and temples, allowing us to express, meditate, explore, heal, and grow. The connection between our minds and bodies is direct; pain in one affects the other. When we prioritize the care of our bodies, we send a message to our souls that we are important. In doing so, we create a safe and supportive environment for our trauma to settle, process, and heal.

> "Eat in Moderation. Live in Moderation. Your Temple is What You Consume"
> *Michelle Belle*

It is possible to transform the mundane act of eating into a meaningful ritual that promotes healing. By dedicating time to nourish, sustain, and elevate our bodies, we can cultivate a space of acceptance and embrace.

Maintaining a healthy diet is not only beneficial to our physical appearance but also to our emotional well-being. Shedding extra weight can help us let go of past pain or stress. Altering our food choices can demonstrate our commitment to self-care and the conscious consumption of nutrients.

There is a strong connection between our bodies, minds, and souls that we often overlook. This isn't just a guide on healthy eating but a holistic approach to healing that involves physical movement, mental and spiritual well-being, and releasing internal traumas. The ultimate goal is to heal your inner sanctuary.

And it all begins in our guts.

Our gut health is the root of our overall well-being. It impacts our mood, mental health, inflammation, and immunity.

Serotonin (the 'happy neurotransmitter') is one of the essential messengers in our bodies. It helps regulate various bodily functions such as emotions, focus, behavior, sleep, digestion, healing, sex drive, blood flow, and breathing.

Did you know that nearly 90% of our body's serotonin is produced in our gut, according to research?

Did you know that 90% of our physical and mental well-being originates from what we consume through our stomachs? It's true, we truly are what we eat.

If you're feeling overwhelmed, take a deep breath. We can't control everything in life, but we can control what we eat. To take charge of your health, begin by looking after your gut.

Imagine your gut as a garden that needs some care and attention. The soil of this garden is your intestinal environment, where over 100 trillion microbial cells reside. The seeds of this garden are the beneficial bacteria that keep it healthy.

To ensure the health and growth of your garden, it is essential to provide the seeds and soil with proper nutrients. One helpful fertilizer is prebiotics, which can help reduce inflammation. Oats, bananas, lentils, asparagus, and even coffee are rich in prebiotics and can benefit your plants.

Did you know that probiotics function like the flowers in your garden? They help protect our bodies and support our immune system.

It's essential to be mindful of consuming unhealthy substances like sugars, alcohol, and caffeine, as they can be likened to weeds that can overtake our system. Allowing these substances to dominate can worsen mood disorders, depression, anxiety, and inflammation. They can also impede our growth and healing by interfering with the communication needed to manage our moods, recovery, and bodily functions.

Let's work together to cultivate this garden and establish a vibrant, flourishing, and harmonious the inner sanctuary that nurtures our healing center. We'll learn how to tend to it with care and commitment.

JOURNAL

Please respond to each prompt and take out a separate journal with a minimum of 1-3 paragraphs. Allow yourself enough time to contemplate, make meaningful connections, and become inspired.

TRUST YOUR GUT

What specific nutrients or dietary components provide power, energy, and alignment in the human body, and which foods are rich sources of these nutrients?

What are some common dietary factors or specific foods known to potentially cause lethargy, lack of focus, or hindered performance, and how can they be avoided or minimized in a balanced diet?

JOURNAL

What are the long-term benefits of prioritizing one's body and health, and how can this mindset positively impact various aspects of life?

_____
_____
_____
_____
_____
_____
_____

What specific goals or motivations do you have for eating healthy, and how do you plan to align your intentions with your actions to maintain a consistent and fulfilling approach toward your dietary choices?

_____
_____
_____
_____
_____
_____
_____
_____

What practical strategies or mindful practices can help transform your mealtime experience from your present routine into a meaningful and enjoyable ritual that enhances your overall well-being and connection with food?

_____
_____
_____
_____
_____
_____
_____
_____

SACRED SIPS SMOOTHIE

CLEANSE YOUR GUT

To promote a healthy gut, starting with a cleanse is important. This involves removing toxins and creating a fresh foundation for optimal gut health. One effective way to do this is by incorporating the Sacred Smoothie into your morning routine three times a week. It's a delicious way to kick-start your day and support your overall health.

Cleanse Your Gut Ingredients:

- 3 tablespoons of SEA MOSS
- Sea Moss Should be blended 1st w/water 2- Frozen Bananas
- 2 cups of Wild Blueberries
- 1/2 cup Pineapple Juice or
- 1/2 cup Alkaline Water
- Two teaspoons of Spirulina
- 1/2 teaspoon of Cinnamon
- Two frozen ginger cubes
- 1/4 scoop of Barley Grass Powder
- 1/4 handful Organic Dulse Leaf
- 1/4 scoop Amla Powder

BLEND 2 MINUTES

LESSON 2

Ayurveda:
The Art Of Eating Healthy

OBJECTIVE:
To explore the gut-brain connection and create a healing inner sanctuary.

A NOTE OF LOVE

Health isn't just a science — it's an art.

But we aim to revolutionize this notion.

Our understanding of health shouldn't be confined to merely what we can observe and measure. True health transcends empirical evidence, embracing the nuanced interplay between physical, mental, emotional, and spiritual selves. Within this broader perspective, Ayurveda, an ancient holistic system of medicine from India, finds its rightful place.

An essential teaching of Ayurveda lies in the balance between spirituality and our human experience. It contends that our spiritual essence and day-to-day experiences aren't separate but deeply interconnected. We must foster this connection for profound contentment, health, and love. We find deeper meaning in life by nurturing our spiritual side and aligning with our higher purpose. And by respecting our human nature – taking care of our bodies and acknowledging our emotions – we align with life's natural ebb and flow. We find the blueprint for holistic well-being and deep fulfillment within this delicate balance.

The profound secret of holistic well-being lies in the dance between the tangible and intangible, between science and art. As we embrace the teachings of Ayurveda and integrate them into our lives, we don't just exist — we thrive. Every meal, every thought, every breath becomes an act of reverence, a testament to the balance of life. It beckons us to ask: Are we merely living or artfully thriving?

"It is in balancing your spirituality with your humanity that you will find immeasurable happiness, success, good health, and love."

— Steve Maraboli

Within the ancient wisdom of Ayurveda lies the understanding that our wellness reflects the world around us, encompassing the five foundational elements: air, water, space, fire, and earth. When these elements intermingle, they give birth to doshas, vital energies that balance and shape our health in distinct ways:

- **Pitta dosha** (fire & water) governs our appetite, thirst, and body temperature.
- **Vata dosha** (air & space) orchestrates our movement and the harmony of our electrolytes.
- **Kapha dosha** (earth & water) fortifies our joints and physical structure.

We each possess a dominant dosha, a blueprint that reveals the specific nutrients and minerals our bodies need to maintain equilibrium.

But Ayurveda teaches us more than just the physicality of health. It reminds us that everything in the Universe, including our food, thrums with energy. These energies interlace, rise, and fall in diverse rhythms, creating a symphony of experiences.

The Ayurvedic tradition identifies three primary energy types or Gunas:

- **Sattva,** embodies pure consciousness.

Mindful, present, and nurturing, it's the essence of the 'Pause.' Sattvic foods are raw, ripe, and fresh ingredients, like plants and elements from the earth:
- Fresh fruits, vegetables, and herbs and Whole grains
- Cheese
- Nuts and seeds
- Honey

- **Rajas**, the catalyst of change.

It's a dynamic force fueling enthusiasm and passion. Rajas foods include potent ingredients such as:
- Meat and fish
- Spices
- Fresh vegetables

- **Tamas**, represents darkness, inaction, and lethargy. The right balance can provide exhalation and groundedness, but too much can cause us to feel heavy, weighed down, and slow. Avoid this sensation by finding balance in tamas foods such as:
- Refined flour
- Fried foods
- Sugary drinks and candies.
- Alcohol, Tobacco Preservatives

As you venture further into the world of Ayurvedic eating, take a moment to Pause, Observe, and Discern. Reflect on the energies you naturally align with. The goal isn't tallying our strengths and weaknesses but cultivating a harmonious dance with our food and, in turn, our essence.

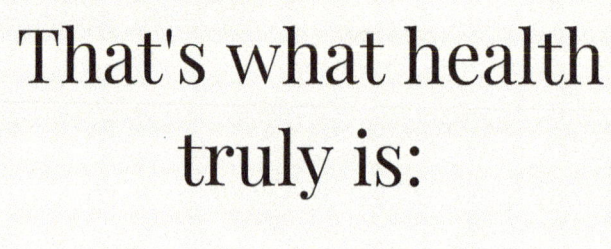

That's what health truly is:

Finding balance

JOURNAL

Please answer each prompt while in a meditative state. Allow yourself enough time to reflect, connect, and receive inspiration. Once you have completed the prompts, you can take a Dosha quiz online.

Meeting Your Body's Inner Healer

As every dosha combines the five elements (air, water, space, fire, earth), which elements are present in your life? How might a deeper connection or balance with these elements enhance your holistic well-being?

_____
_____
_____

With the understanding that everything carries energy, especially food, how might adopting a more conscious eating approach transform your physical health and mental and spiritual equilibrium?

_____
_____
_____

Think of a timewhen you felt out of balance. Which dosha or guna may have been dominant then? How can this insight help you in addressing future imbalances?

_____
_____
_____

> *Our souls are always in transition. The more we embrace grounding in our lives, the more we tune into the PAUSE of our true alignment.*
>
> — Michele Bell

JOURNAL

Please answer each prompt while in a meditative state. Allow yourself time to reflect, connect, and receive inspiration. Once you have completed the prompts, you may take a Dosha quiz online.

Connecting to Your Inner Sanctuary

Considering the unique energies of the doshas and gunas, which do you feel resonates most with your current state? How can understanding this dominant energy guide your path to healing and balance?

Reflecting on the foods associated with each energy type (Sattva, Rajas, Tamas), which ones do you naturally gravitate towards? How might aligning your diet with your dominant dosha foster not just physical but emotional and spiritual well-being?

Envision a future where you've harmonized with the Ayurvedic principles daily. What changes do you see in your mental, emotional, and physical health? How will this harmony influence your overall perspective on wellness and healing?

FOREST BATHING
journal prompts

Practicing writing as mindfulness can be highly helpful in preventing the build-up of overwhelming information in our minds.

Preventing us from becoming "clogged" in the channels of our mind, which over time can lead to states like brain fog, overwhelm and burnout, memory loss, insomnia, and—of course—various forms of indigestion in the gut.

Incorporating writing into your mindfulness routine can be valuable for self-discovery and growth. However, it's crucial to acknowledge the impact of the doshas on your thoughts and expression. Your constitution, current imbalances, time of day, and stage of life all play a role in determining which dosha is dominant. You can identify and work towards balancing your mental and physical elements using prompts. Before commencing with your writing practice, it's recommended to take a moment to center yourself through meditation or bodily movements. Afterward, find a peaceful spot under a tree, grab a notebook, and allow your thoughts to flow freely onto the page.

FOREST BATHING
journal prompts

VATA

Choose a body part that you feel neutral about emotionally and physically. Please write a letter to that body part and share what you appreciate about it. Set a timer for 5 to 15 minutes and only write within the limits of this creative container.

PITTA

Close your eyes and take three breaths before you sit down to write and clear the surrounding space. If you wish, light a candle or incense, or apply some essential oil or perfume to invite in a fragrance you enjoy. Open your notebook so you see two facing pages (left-hand and right-hand side), and let your writing only fill that space—stop when you fill those two pages. Write about a childhood feeling-free and playful memory, or draw or doodle any associated feelings or memories. Close your eyes and take three breaths before moving into your next activity.

KAPHA

Relocate to a comfortable spot with pillows, blankets, or a cup of tea. Set a timer for 5 to 15 minutes and jot down a list of the qualities you appreciate about yourself, your daily routine, or your present life. Keep your descriptions brief, limiting each to one line on the page. Maintain continuous writing throughout the session. Once finished, read your list aloud and select one item or activity to incorporate into your day.

JOURNAL

How have lingering thoughts or emotions clouded your mind lately? Can you pinpoint times when mental clutter led to stress or physical symptoms?

Reflect on your dosha. How do your dominant dosha's characteristics influence how you process thoughts and emotions? Have you noticed any patterns or shifts in your mental clarity or well-being when aligning with practices tailored to your dosha?

SACRED SIPS SMOOTHIE

SATTVIC SMOOTHIE

To kick-start the process, let's focus on purifying your gut. This involves eliminating harmful toxins and nurturing a strong foundation for optimal gut health. One effective way to achieve this is by incorporating the Sacred Smoothie into your morning routine twice weekly.

Sattvic Smoothie Ingredients:

- 3 tablespoons of Mele Moss
- 1 cup Wild Blueberries 1/4 Avocado
- 1/2 cup of Frozen Mango 1/2 Frozen Kiwi
- 1/2 cup Frozen Fresh Strawberries
- 1 cup of Kale or Spinach
- 1 tsp of Cinnamon
- 1 cup Coconut Water
- 1 frozen ginger cube
- 6 Mint Leaves
- 1/4 scoop Haritaki powder
- 1 tsp Flax seed

BLEND 2 MINUTES

LESSON 3

Find the Right Diet for You

OBJECTIVE:
Explore different diets, tune into your bodily needs, and find foods that fuel your wellness.

A NOTE OF LOVE

Demystifying the 'Diet'

As humans, we overcomplicate things... a lot.

Dieting is an area that we have made unnecessarily complex. Our focus on health has become overly compartmentalized, compromised, and commercialized, leading to diet trends. Carbs, for instance, are deemed good one year and bad the next. Similarly, grapefruit is recommended for breakfast one year, and then bacon and eggs the next.

What's the solution? It's actually the opposite of following trends: Simplify things.

> *A Journey of a Thousand Moments Begins with a Spoonful of Wellness.*
>
> — Michelle Bell

We can find the nutrients we need all around us on the earth. There's no need to spend a fortune on trendy diets and products when we can opt for whole foods. One such dietary approach is the Whole Food, Plant-Based (WFPB) diet, which emphasizes natural foods like fruits, vegetables, whole grains, and legumes while limiting heavily processed and animal-based ingredients.

This diet can transform our lives, backed by scientific research and ancient wisdom. It can improve our mood, energy levels, and skin, reduce inflammation, lower cholesterol, and regulate our hormones. By reducing our risk of diabetes, heart disease, and other chronic illnesses, we can achieve a more balanced and elevated state of being.

Ultimately, it all starts with our mindset and thought process.

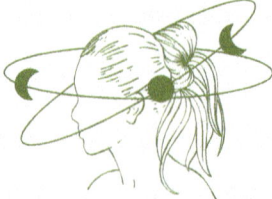

Many of us overcomplicate dieting by believing there's only one method, one diet, and one answer for our health. But we both understand this is a misconception spread by inadequate advertising and a lack of open-mindedness.

We must learn to tune into our minds and bodies to combat it. One effective method is to identify what our bodies require by using the POD method through:

Expressing, Meditating, Being Present, Rejuvenating, Awakening, Connecting, and Eating Healthy.

When you take the time to listen to your body's cues — and give it what it needs — you initiate the healing process. You show your body that it matters. That you matter.

Throughout my wellness journey, I have discovered that gluten and dairy hinder my overall health. So, I have made it a priority to avoid them. Since implementing this change, I have noticed a significant improvement in my health, particularly after my caregiver responsibilities. My daily goal is to avoid these foods to maintain my newfound well-being.

My suggestion is always that it's all in moderation. Balance is the key to creating JOY in the journey. Find a routine that acts as a ritual for your health, reminding you to be present, tune in, and fuel your mind, body, and spiritual well-being.

Some individuals strive to discover a nutrition plan that caters to their specific body and blood type. According to naturopathic research, consuming meals corresponding to your blood type can enhance overall health and well-being by promoting greater alignment.

- Type O Blood: Eat high-protein foods, lean meats, fish, and vegetables.
- Type A: Eat plant-based, focusing on fresh, organic fruits and vegetables.
- Type B: Eat leafy greens, eggs, low-fat dairy, no gluten, nuts, corn, and seeds.
- Type AB: Eat fresh seafood, tofu, dairy, and leafy greens, avoiding caffeine.

No matter where your journey takes you, prioritize creating a harmonious and supportive environment in your gut for optimal health. Remember that your gut microbiome is vital for mental and physical well-being. It's home to trillions of microorganisms that work together to support your digestion, immune system, and mental health. Nourish it with healthy bacteria such as probiotics.

- Miso
- Kombucha
- Kimchi
- Tempeh

> *The abundance of super-centric food on our planet is truly a remarkable gift that can provide us with the healing properties we need.*
>
> *Michele Bell*

JOURNAL

Please respond to the prompts below after each meal today. This guide will serve as a reminder for you to check in with your body and listen to its needs.

Find the Right Diet for You.

What are the key benefits and long-term impacts of maintaining a healthy diet on my overall well-being and quality of life?
_____
_____
_____

Considering my current eating habits, what steps can I take to enhance my overall diet and incorporate healthier choices into my daily routine?
_____
_____
_____
_____

How do you feel when you eat red meat? Sugar? Dairy? (Create a personalized menu if enrolled in the certified course.)
_____
_____
_____
_____

JOURNAL

Answer the following prompts after each meal today. Use this as a guide and reminder to check in and listen to your body:

I invite you to schedule a consultation with me to explore your options for healthy eating and discover ways to feel energized.

Do you prefer fruit or vegetables or both? Why?

_____
_____
_____

How important is it for you to have a connection with your eating habits?

_____
_____
_____

Write a poem expressing the significance of maintaining a healthy diet to your younger self vs. present moment.

_____
_____
_____
_____
_____
_____
_____
_____

> *Your soul is the center of your Universe.*
> *Nurturing it will nourish your inner sanctuary.*

CHOPPED MEDLEY– HEALTHY TAPAS BOWL

To maintain their distinct flavors and textures, it's best to cook barley and freekeh separately, each taking about 30 minutes. Don't worry; you can cook them ahead of time and refrigerate them for a day or two before assembling the dish. Once the grains are cooked, it's easy to put everything together. This salad is sturdy enough for a buffet table and can be covered and refrigerated for several days, but it's fluffiest when consumed within a day or two. You can serve it warm or at room temperature.

For the Salad:

- 1 cup wheat berries (or freekeh or barley)
- ½ teaspoon salt or to taste
- 1 orange
- 1 avocado
- ½ cup dates, chopped
- ½ cup figs, chopped
- ½ cup white or red grapes halved
- ½ small red onion, chopped fine
- ½ cup olives, chopped
- ½ cup pomegranate seeds
- 2-4 red cabbage leaves
- 5 scallions or green onions, sliced thin
- 1 cup toasted pecans (or pistachios)
- 1 cup feta cheese (optional)

For the Dressing:

- ¼ cup balsamic vinegar
- 1 clove garlic, minced
- 1 teaspoon manuka honey
- 1/4 teaspoon bee pollen
- ½ teaspoon dry mustard
- Sea Salt and ground pepper to taste
- ¼ cup extra virgin olive oil

To prepare a delicious grain dish, fill a medium-sized saucepan with water. Next, add wheat berries and half a teaspoon of salt. Bring the mixture to a boil and let it simmer for an hour or until the grains reach an al dente consistency. Once done, drain the grains and rinse them under cold water to halt the cooking process. Transfer them to a bowl and allow them to cool completely.

Start by placing the cabbage on a flat plate and sprinkling wheat berries. Next, carefully peel the oranges and slice them between the sections before adding them to the salad. Add avocado, dates, figs, grapes, red onions, olives, pomegranate seeds, scallions, pecans, and feta cheese. Finally, drizzle some dressing over the salad, toss it all together, and serve on top of cabbage leaves.

MINDFUL EATING
tips

When it comes to our well-being, we are not just bodies with souls or souls with bodies. We must look at the body and soul together as one. There is unity between our body and soul — no matter how deeply we tune in to our spiritual practice, we also need to focus on human health-- and how we fuel our bodies. Food does not just fuel the body but the soul as well. We are this unity.

Practice taking a few moments to sit with the food before you eat it—just a few breaths to take it all in with your senses and prepare for eating.

Eat slowly, making it a point to put the silverware down after every few bites and sit back. This can take some willpower. The payoff is that as your practice of attentive eating grows, you will stop eating when you begin to feel complete. The indicator of fullness is the first belch. This signifies the stomach is letting out some air to make space for the food—so if you add more food, your stomach will run out of room. Eat slowly enough to notice the belch, and you will find it's your body's built-in system for portion control!

Try different breakfast portions over a few weeks to find the ideal amount that keeps you satiated until lunchtime, eliminating the need for snacking. Establishing a consistent mealtime routine can assist you in accomplishing this goal. It's typically more difficult to resist snacking in the afternoon than in the morning.

As you settle into a breakfast and lunch routine, paying attention to how much food you need to feel satiated until dinner is a good idea. Take note if you skip lunch and snack on sweets or coffee throughout the afternoon. To avoid this, packing a satisfying lunch can help keep you fueled and focused.

LESSON 4

The Spiritual Cleanse of Fasting

OBJECTIVE:
To explore the physical, mental, and spiritual benefits of fasting, what it symbolizes, and how to practice it.

A NOTE OF LOVE

Reset Your Inner Rhythm

Rethinking Health and Healing: The Benefits of Fasting

Many believe the latest diet, supplements, and trendy recipes are key to our health and healing. However, fasting can effectively support personal growth, self-awareness, and spiritual development along our journey.

Fasting has physical and spiritual benefits when maintaining a healthy diet. Physically, fasting can reset the body and digestive system, allowing it to rest and heal. It can also promote fat burning, improve metabolic flexibility, and regulate insulin levels.

> *Practice discernment in moderation through faith and promise honoring our inner sanctuary. It will all come together.*
>
> *Michelle Bell*

The Spiritual Benefits of Fasting Across Different Belief Systems

Fasting is a sacred practice that has been observed in various cultures and faiths throughout human history. By detaching from material aspects and focusing on spiritual growth, fasting promotes self-discipline, mindfulness, and a stronger connection with oneself and spiritual beliefs. Let's explore how fasting is observed in different belief systems:

- In the 5th century B.C., Hippocrates recommended fasting as a healing practice.
- During Lent, several Christian denominations practice fasting.
- Many Buddhists fast daily, from noon until dawn.
- Muslims observe Ramadan, a month of fasting, prayer, and reflection.
- In Judaism, members honor Yom Kippur by fasting from sundown to sundown.
- In Hindu and Jain cultures, Ekadashi is observed twice a month, where individuals fast in sync with the lunar cycle.

Regardless of culture or belief system, fasting has been shown to provide significant spiritual benefits.

Awakening through Abstinence

Exploring the Transformative Benefits

Increased mindfulness: Fasting requires a conscious effort to refrain from eating during specific periods. Mindfulness and self-discipline can extend beyond food and cultivate a greater awareness of one's thoughts, emotions, and actions in everyday life. It can help in breaking habitual patterns and promoting present-moment awareness.

Heightened spiritual focus: Fasting can create a conducive environment for spiritual practices, such as meditation, prayer, or introspection. By abstaining from food, one can redirect their attention inward, fostering a deeper connection with their inner self and spiritual beliefs. This focused state can facilitate a sense of clarity, insight, and spiritual connection.

Detachment from material desires: Fasting involves willingly letting go of physical desires and attachments, including the desire for food. This practice of detachment can extend to other areas of life, helping individuals cultivate a healthier relationship with material possessions, cravings, and external dependencies. It encourages a shift towards valuing inner qualities, virtues, and spiritual growth over external gratification.

Purification and rejuvenation: Fasting is often associated with cleansing and purifying the body. By giving the digestive system a break, the body can redirect its energy toward healing, repair, and detoxification. This physical purification can be seen as symbolic of purifying the mind, emotions, and spirit, creating space for personal growth, emotional release, and spiritual transformation.

Heightened sensitivity and intuition: Fasting may enhance sensory perception and intuitive abilities. With a lighter body and a clearer mind, individuals may experience heightened sensitivity to their surroundings, increased intuition, and a deeper connection with their inner guidance. This can support decision-making, intuition-based practices, and greater alignment with oneself.

EMBRACE the wisdom of your body and inner guidance, approaching fasting with mindfulness, moderation, and self-care as you honor your well-being. Through the harmonious integration of practices aligned with your true self, nourish the divine connection within and continue to pivot with purpose on a profound journey of self-discovery. You Got This, Warrior!

Unlocking Transformation

Fasting holds an intimate discipline that can guide you to higher levels of consciousness and deep inner healing. Through this practice, you cultivate strength and gain control over your appetite. Combine this newfound discipline with our Be Present - Pause - Observe and Discernment journey techniques within these writings, and you'll unlock resistance.

Fasting becomes a sacred gateway to elevated states of consciousness. By consciously abstaining from food, you create space for introspection, silence, and heightened awareness. This **PAUSE** reveals a deep connection with your inner self and the divine presence within and around you. Observing the workings of your mind, emotions, and desires during fasting brings clarity and a broader perspective that transcends the ordinary.

Alongside fasting, embrace the power of **PAUSE** in each moment, and cultivating mindfulness anchors you in the present reality, freeing you from attachment to past regrets and future anxieties. Through this lifestyle, you fully immerse yourself in the beauty and richness of every experience, discovering wisdom and healing in the simplest of moments.

Discernment becomes an invaluable companion on this transformative journey. You discern choices and influences, consciously selecting what aligns with your higher self and purpose. Fasting, combined with discernment, refines desires and empowers you to make conscious choices that support your overall well-being and spiritual growth.

EMBRACE the intimate essence of fasting, allowing it to unlock the depths of your being. Combine it with mindful presence and discerning wisdom. Through this synergy, you'll re-posture your purpose-discovery journey, access higher consciousness, and experience deep inner healing. May you open your heart to the divine guidance within your "decided life."

Fasting Modalities

Intermittent Time-Restricted Fasting

As creatures of habit, we develop a natural inclination to live, work, rest, and sleep according to a specific routine. This kind of fasting involves aligning our "internal clocks". Our mealtimes are crucial in regulating this clock. When we eat late or at irregular intervals, our bodies become disoriented, making it challenging to sleep, wake up, or stay energized when required.

Aiming to consume your meals within an 8-12 hour window every day could promote a more natural rhythm for your body, ultimately enhancing your overall health and well-being.

Intermittent Calorie-Restricted Fasting

One method of fasting centers around the number of calories or energy we consume each day. With intermittent calorie restriction, you reduce your calorie intake by 50% for two days, followed by five days of normal eating. This approach offers a weekly reset, promoting bodily cleansing and mental clarity.

Periodic Fasting

This type of fasting encourages you to limit your calories for 3-5 consecutive days during the month, eating normally for the rest.

You regain more control and intention as you find what works for your body. You become more mindful of what you eat, how you feel, and how you want to feel.

SACRED SIPS SMOOTHIE

When breaking your fast, it's important to approach it with the same mindfulness level as when fasting. Begin with nourishing foods that will set a positive tone for your day. Consider alternating between the recipes provided in previous chapters three times a week.

INTENTIONAL BREAK-FAST SMOOTHIE

- 1 tbsp of SEA MOSS
- 1 tbsp of Peanut Butter
- 1 cup of Frozen Wild Blueberries
- 1 Frozen Banana
- 1/4 scoop Haritaki powder
- 1/4 tsp Cinnamon
- 1 tsp Flax Seed
- 1/4 scoop Amla powder
- 1/4 scoop Barley Grass Powder
- 1 tsp Cocoa Powder
- 1 cup Unsweetened Almond/Oat Milk

BLEND 2 MINUTES

LESSON 5

Mindful Eating:
Embrace the Present Nourish the Soul

OBJECTIVE:
To navigate the meaning of mindful eating, its benefits, and how to practice it in your daily life.

A NOTE OF LOVE
Enjoy the Moment

We've all done it:

We grab a protein bar and rush out the door in the morning. We often rush through meals, unaware of what we eat —distracted by screens and obligations. But how often do we genuinely savor the act of eating?

Amidst the chaos, daily rituals serve as anchors, providing stability in an ever-changing world. And what better ritual to bring us back to the present than the one we repeat three times a day? Mindful eating is a profound practice encompassing the physical, emotional, and spiritual realms, grounding us in the here and now.

When we engage in mindful eating, we awaken our senses and rediscover the joys of the daily human experience.

It is a powerful reminder to nourish our bodies and connect with food's flavors and sensations. Even on the most challenging days, mindful eating becomes an act of self-care. Being present for our meals, listening to our body's cues, and honoring its nourishment can provide solace and comfort.

Mindful eating goes beyond a mere buzzword; it is an intentional practice. It invites us to make conscious decisions about what we eat and when. It encourages us to listen to our bodies, disregarding social expectations and time constraints. With mindful eating, we sit down and fully experience each bite and sip, tuning in to our hunger and honoring our satisfaction.

> By embracing mindful eating, we nourish our soul, finding a pause moment amidst the chaos allowing ascension to consume our inner sanctuary.
>
> *Michelle Bell*

THE POWER OF PAUSE

Above all, it's about taking a moment to pause. You know the Power of the Pause if you've gone through all the EMBRACE modalities with us. A Pause between each bite allows your body time and space for digestion. It will enable you to enjoy the textures and tastes. It sets the tone for intention. A Pause at mealtime can extend into the rest of your day, encouraging you to Pause and be present throughout the rest of your life.

Let this be your guide as you begin to take a Pause of Power with each meal:

- Start by focusing on how you're feeling both physically and emotionally. Identify the nourishment that would benefit you the most right now.

- Listen to your body. If you feel full, stop eating and save the remaining food for later. This fosters a healthier connection between your mind and body.

- Savor every bite. After each bite, pay attention to your sensory experience — the flavors, aromas, and textures.

- Prepare your food with intention. This could mean shopping at a farmer's market, cooking meals from scratch, or simply taking a few moments before each meal to pause and reconnect with the food in front of you.

- Eat with the sole focus of nourishing yourself. Allow yourself time to eat without distractions. Turn off the TV or put away your phone.

- Create rituals around meals. This could be as simple as lighting a candle before eating or setting an intention for the meal. This helps create a sense of sacredness around what is usually seen as a mundane task.

- Check-in with your body. Observe how different foods make you feel, and trust yourself enough to listen to your body signals -- provide what it needs.

Mindful eating paves the way to presence. It inspires us to slow down, savor it all, and appreciate the nourishment we're receiving. It empowers our connection with ourselves, strengthening our ability to tune in and provide for our needs.

So, savor every bite — and every moment.

JOURNAL

Answer these prompts at the end of your next meal:

Savor it All

What did I eat? Describe the tastes, textures, and sensations.

How do I physically feel at this very moment?

How do I emotionally feel at this very moment

JOURNAL

How might the simple act of pausing influence the quality of your meal and your day? How can you apply the Power of the Pause elsewhere in your life?

_____
_____
_____
_____
_____
_____
_____
_____
_____

Write a heartfelt note to your body, expressing your deep appreciation for its remarkable ability to transform your meals into sustenance and vitality.

_____
_____
_____
_____
_____
_____
_____
_____
_____

SACRED SIPS & SNACKS CHALLENGE

Today, you will create your recipe by mindfully tuning into your body and needs. Ask yourself:

- Does my body need vegetables right now? If so, which ones?
- Does my body need fruits right now? If so, which ones?
- Does my body need grains right now? If so, which ones?
- Does my body need proteins right now? If so, which ones?
- Does my body need fats right now? If so, which ones?

Recipe for My Sacred Sip or Snack Warrior Blend

_____
_____
_____
_____
_____
_____
_____

Create a grocery list based on your answers, and intentionally plan meals that fuel your needs. Listen to the Eat Healthy Meditation during this exercise.

LESSON 6

EMBRACE forward

OBJECTIVE:
To combine the seven EMBRACE modalities altogether, aligning our journey for continued healing, growth, and grace

A NOTE OF LOVE

EMBRACING WHAT HAS, WHAT IS, & WHAT WILL BE.

Congratulations, my wellness warrior — you've arrived. Blessed be your journey.

Eat Healthy may be the final modality in the **EMBRACE** journey, but it's only the beginning.

As we close this final chapter, I want you to begin a new story. But this time? You're the author. You're the main character. You get to decide what direction you're heading.
While you may anticipate only some plot twists, conflicts, and cliffhangers ahead, you can choose your perspective. Through the lens of **EMBRACE**, you can decide to **EXPRESS** your raw emotions, explore your endless imagination, and expand your powerful authenticity.

You can soothe the scars and pains of grief through **MEDITATION**. By tapping into your inner healing abilities, you can cultivate hope, **EMBRACE** them, and find the balance between positive and negative emotions.

When you feel caught between past pain and future fear, take a moment to embrace the pause and **BE "fully" PRESENT**. Ground yourself in the peace and stillness of the current moment.

You can raise your vibrations and **REJUVENATE** your energy to embark on a new healing path. You can honor your loved ones, yourself, and your journey with rituals of self-care and self-love.

You can remind yourself of the magic of being here now and **AWAKEN** your soul's purpose. You can envision your healing, connect to your Source Energy, and reignite each breath with renewed abundance.

When you feel lost, you can find your roots and **CONNECT** with your inner child, wisdom, and joy. You can grow and evolve by releasing what no longer serves you, making peace with your pain, and strengthening your relationship with yourself.

Lastly, it's essential to prioritize **EAT HEALTHY**—nourishing your mind and body. This will give you the necessary energy to:
        Express, Meditate, Be Present, Rejuvenate, Awaken, and Connect.

THE POD

Pause Observe Discern

The POD modality, consisting of Pause, Observe, and Discern, offers a powerful framework to navigate your journey with intention and self-awareness.
Let's explore how each element can be incorporated into your life during this transformative process:

Pause: Taking intentional moments of pause allows you to create space for reflection. Examples of incorporating pause may include:
- Carving out dedicated time each day for quiet contemplation.
- Stepping away from the busyness of daily life.
- Prioritizing self-care practices that replenish your energy.

Observe: Cultivating the skill of observation helps you become more aware of your thoughts, emotions, and the patterns that arise during your journey.
Examples of incorporating observation into your life may include:
- Mindfully noticing your feelings as they arise without judgment or suppression, allowing yourself to experience and process them fully.
- Journaling to explore your thoughts, emotions, and any insights that arise during your grieving process.
- Paying attention to physical sensations in your body, such as tension or discomfort, and using this awareness to guide self-care and relaxation practices.
-

Discern: Discernment involves making conscious decisions based on your inner wisdom. Examples of incorporating discernment into your life may include:
- Practicing self-compassion and allowing yourself to set boundaries with activities or people that may not serve your healing process.
- Seeking support from trusted individuals, such as friends, family, or professionals, and discerning whom to share your journey with based on their empathy and understanding.
- Make choices about how to honor and remember your loved one, whether through rituals, creating a memory keepsake, or engaging in significant activities for you.

Remember, the POD modality is a guide to support you on your unique grief journey. As you incorporate Pause, Observe, and Discern, adapt and personalize these practices to align with your needs and values. Embrace the power of the POD modality as a tool for self-discovery, healing, and growth during this transformative time.

INTUITIVE PROMPTS

Embracing is more than simply accepting our circumstances. It's far more than "moving on" or "letting go." To EMBRACE is to carve out space for both the positive and negative aspects of life and everything in between. It's embracing and accepting our most profound, darkest moments with presence and patience. It's embracing and buckling up for the rollercoaster journey of grief.

Even more?

It's pivoting from this pain to find our purpose. It's turning toward our grief and giving ourselves grace. It's honoring our loss and cultivating love.

It's time to pick up your journal!

1. How will I honor the essence of EXPRESSION as I move forward?
a. What unique ways can I give voice to my emotions, thoughts, and experiences?
b. Why is it essential for me to authentically express myself on this journey?

2. How will I embrace the art of MEDITATION as I move forward?
a. What practices or techniques can I explore to cultivate inner stillness and clarity?
b. Why do I recognize the significance of creating space for peaceful reflection?

3. How will I wholeheartedly embrace the magic of BEING PRESENT as I move *with*?
a. What mindful rituals or practices can I incorporate into my daily life?
b. Why is it crucial for me to fully immerse myself in the beauty of each moment?

4. How will I nourish my soul and REJUVENATE as I continue?
a. What self-care rituals bring me a sense of deep rejuvenation and renewal?
b. Why do I recognize the importance of restoring my energy and finding balance?

5. How will I AWAKEN my inner spirit and embrace the limitless possibilities ahead?
a. What steps can I take to awaken my passions, dreams, and potential?
b. Why do I believe in the transformative power of embracing my true calling?

6. How will I foster CONNECTION with myself and others as I progress?
a. What practices or actions can deepen my connections?
b. Why should I value the power of genuine connections on this growth journey?

7. How will I prioritize the gift of EATING HEALTHY as I continue my path?
a. What healthy choices and habits will I cultivate to honor my body and mind?
b. What changes can I expect to see in my overall health as a result of maintaining a balanced and nutritious diet?

Embrace your intuitive power and reflect on these prompts as you ascend, weaving your unique story of growth and transformation.

— HEALING IT FORWARD —

i am so proud of you

Reflect on your EMBRACE journey. If you haven't yet, read all seven books and modalities of EMBRACE to align your path forward.

Use your Journal Prompt answers to create a plan and commit to EMBRACE daily, "Healing it Forward."

Moving through grief is a challenging task. From the initial shock to the following sadness and emptiness, allowing yourself to go through it all can be difficult. But embracing our feelings and being willing to move with them will eventually bring us more joy. This gives us a heartfelt chance to honor our loved ones until we embrace them again.

The 7 STAGES of GRIEF modalities recognize this challenge and provide structure and support for intentionally moving with grief. Reminding ourselves to PAUSE in reflection during times of sorrow will help us be open to experiencing peace within ourselves, allowing the grace of the grief journey to fill our hearts until we meet those we lost again someday.

SACRED DETOX BATH RECIPES

How Detox Baths Work

Ancient wisdom and modern science combine to provide a therapeutic experience. Through osmosis, hot water draws toxic energy while cooling waters pull it away from your body as you immerse yourself in four cleansing baths - making them an ideal way to enjoy both health benefits and relaxation simultaneously!

Cleansing baths help draw toxins out of the body, allowing one to safely detoxify regularly - up 2-3 times per week with no more than once daily recommended for most people.

Baking Soda Detox Baths

Immerse yourself in an invigorating and therapeutic aluminum-free baking soda bath to help address symptoms related to radiation exposure, swollen glands, sore throats, or gums. Fill your regular-sized tub with as hot water as you can tolerate and dissolve 4 cups of baking soda until completely dissolved. Enjoy a relaxing 45-minute soak, emerging from the bath feeling rejuvenated - no need to rinse off afterward! This refreshing ritual also benefits those suffering from digestive impairments, such as stomach discomfort when digesting food.

SACRED DETOX BATH RECIPES

Epsom Salts Detox Baths

Dissolve 2 cups of Epsom salts (source) in a regular-sized bath. Use more as needed if your tub is oversized. The temperature should be comfortably warm but not overly hot. Soak for at least 12 minutes and up to 20-30 minutes. Rinse and towel dry.

Did you know that the scientific name for Epsom salt is magnesium sulfate? Although magnesium and sulfur are essential nutrients, they may not be efficiently absorbed from our diet. However, soaking in Epsom salts can help solve this issue since these minerals are easily absorbed through the skin. According to the Epsom Salt Industry Council, a simple Epsom salt soak can provide various health benefits, such as improving heart and circulatory health, reducing blood pressure, relieving muscle pain, and eliminating harmful toxins from the body. Additionally, it can enhance nerve function by promoting proper regulation of electrolytes. For general health maintenance or to alleviate the discomfort of bruises and sprains, it's recommended to soak in Epsom salts 2-3 times per week. Moreover, an Epsom salt soak can also aid in detoxifying drugs that remain in the body after surgery.

Sea Salt and Baking Soda Detox Baths

Indulge in a soothing therapeutic bath that helps reduce exposure to environmental radiation, X-rays, plane flights, and airport screenings. Add a pound of sea salt or rock salt to a hot tub filled with warm water and another pound of baking soda. Immerse yourself in the relaxing soak for approximately 45 minutes until the temperature is comfortable, then towel dry without rinsing off. For optimal results, take this bath just before bedtime and enjoy a peaceful slumber after achieving a full-body state of relaxation.

SACRED DETOX BATH RECIPES

Apple Cider Vinegar (ACV) Detox Baths

A natural way to detoxify your body, alleviate muscle aches and pains, and reduce excess uric acid levels is by taking an apple cider vinegar (ACV) bath. To do this, add 2 cups of pure ACV to a hot bath and soak for about 45 minutes. For more oversized baths, adjust the amount of ACV accordingly. Once finished, pat yourself dry and avoid showering or bathing for at least 8 hours. This simple and effective ACV bath can relieve joint pain caused by gout or arthritis and sore muscles after physical activity. Additionally, it can help combat excessive body odor.
(Recommended once a month on a full moon-releasing and letting go!)

Contraindications

Maintaining a regular detox bath routine can significantly benefit your overall well-being. However, it's essential to exercise moderation and caution when preparing your bath. It's recommended to only stick to one formula per day and avoid mixing ingredients from various recipes, as this can lead to unforeseen complications. Additionally, if you are pregnant, it's imperative to consult with your healthcare provider before starting any detox routine. Your healthcare provider can provide guidance and advice to ensure your detox bath is safe and effective. Remember, taking care of your well-being is a top priority, and with careful consideration and proper guidance, you can enjoy the many benefits of a detox bath routine.

A Message of Encouragement for Warriors on the Journey of Life

I want to express my gratitude for embracing life's unpredictable journey. This moment is a testament to your courage and resilience.

Your spirit has evolved throughout this transformative journey of mind, body, and soul. Even if the changes are not immediately apparent, be aware that your energy is shifting and your mindset is reframing. Embrace this renewal and prepare yourself for the profound transformations that lie ahead.

Life is filled with unpredictable twists and turns, but let each surprise be an opportunity to embrace every experience, no matter how unexpected. Choose to create meaning. Choose to move with it, learn from it, or grow from it. Pivot with purpose.

Every morning is a blank canvas, awaiting the masterful strokes of creation. Stop looking at changes as endings but see them as new beginnings. Will you rise to today's challenge and embrace your purpose, honoring your existence?

Remember, you've got this!

Soul Architect
About Michele

Meet Michele, The Grief Warrior® — a title earned from decades of resilience amidst adversity. Her story is of strength, perseverance, and a transformative purpose that binds spiritual depth with authentic, real-world experience.

From an early age, Michele faced challenges that would have daunted many — from bullying to domestic abuse. Yet, her unyielding spirit and unwavering determination saw her through. As a Holistic Real Estate Broker for over 30 years, she guided families in transitions, turning houses into homes. This role wasn't just a profession; it echoed her innate desire to support individuals through life's significant shifts.

In 2001, when her teenage son was diagnosed with Ewings Sarcoma, Michele's commitment as a single mother was tested like never before. She requested a mere 10 hours a week off to care for him. Yet, a prominent NYC developer unfairly dismissed her the next day. With unwavering resolve, as a single mother with no child support, Michele sold real estate from her son's bedside for the last five years of his life.

The loss of her son in 2005 marked a profound turning point. "Moving with" evolved from a personal mantra to a beacon for others navigating their tragedies. This journey, a dream of motherhood cut short, is poignantly captured in her award-winning adapted screenplay, *A Son's Gift*, aka *A Journey of Unconditional Love*.

Her contributions to mental health advocacy are vast and impactful. Michele's groundbreaking methodologies, like the pioneering Soul Design technique and the 7 Stages of Grief workbooks, have brought solace and understanding to many. As a certified suicide prevention advocate and an active member of Domestic Abuse and Violence programs across the Northeast, Michele's voice became a force for change.

In every endeavor, whether as a real estate broker, an end-of-life expert, or a mental health advocate, Michele's purpose is to support, guide, and uplift. As a prominent member of the Daughters of Penelope, one of the oldest women's Philahellenic organizations, she has graced many platforms as a keynote speaker, sharing her inspiring messages of healing, humor, and love, a necessity in today's world.

Now, at 57, while the world may see a seasoned professional, Michele's authenticity commands respect, and the bond is deep, authentic, and unconditional for those fortunate enough to know her truly. To many, she's not just **The Grief Warrior®**; she's a testament to the human spirit and resilience.

Michele, despite her many commendable accolades and achievements, holds that her life experiences have granted her invaluable CAT credentials:

Compassion. Authenticity. Trusting.

Testimonial

My name is Cristal Sampson, and I work in mental health and psychiatry as a nurse practitioner in Connecticut and New York, specializing in traumatic stress and mood disorders. I am also a woman who experienced an early-term spontaneous miscarriage that burned a hole in my depths I had previously not known existed. The revelation of this new depth of unconditional Love, coupled with my baby's teeny heart-stopping, left me hollow.

Even in my subsequent pregnancy the following year, I still felt empty of the unfulfillable desire for the baby back that I had lost in this life. The emptiness was filled with sadness, anxiety, and disappointment from troubled family dynamics – a family unaware of my loss and grief.

Someone like me in the field of my expertise is never immune to the heartaches of the human experience, like loss of love and life. I recognized the potential to be an emotionally absent mother to my unborn baby, which was all but set in stone at the time – and the thought terrified me. I am grateful to have known that I owed my baby and myself the chance to heal. In my research, I found Michele, The Grief Warrior.

As a health professional and a mental health professional, I tend to be incredibly picky about whom I receive services from and what services I seek. At this period in my life and for this circumstance, I did not seek "traditional" mental health counseling. At the time, I could not face modern therapy's issues. I saw the potential for the more traditional route as most helpful later in my healing.

What Michele offered touched the core, breadth, and depth of my hurting, going deep into the spiritual, mental, emotional, and energetic spaces of my being, body, and surroundings through a one-on-one retreat. I've experienced nothing like it since, so I am glad you are here reading Caregiver 101. I know that your experience will change you with Michele through this book.

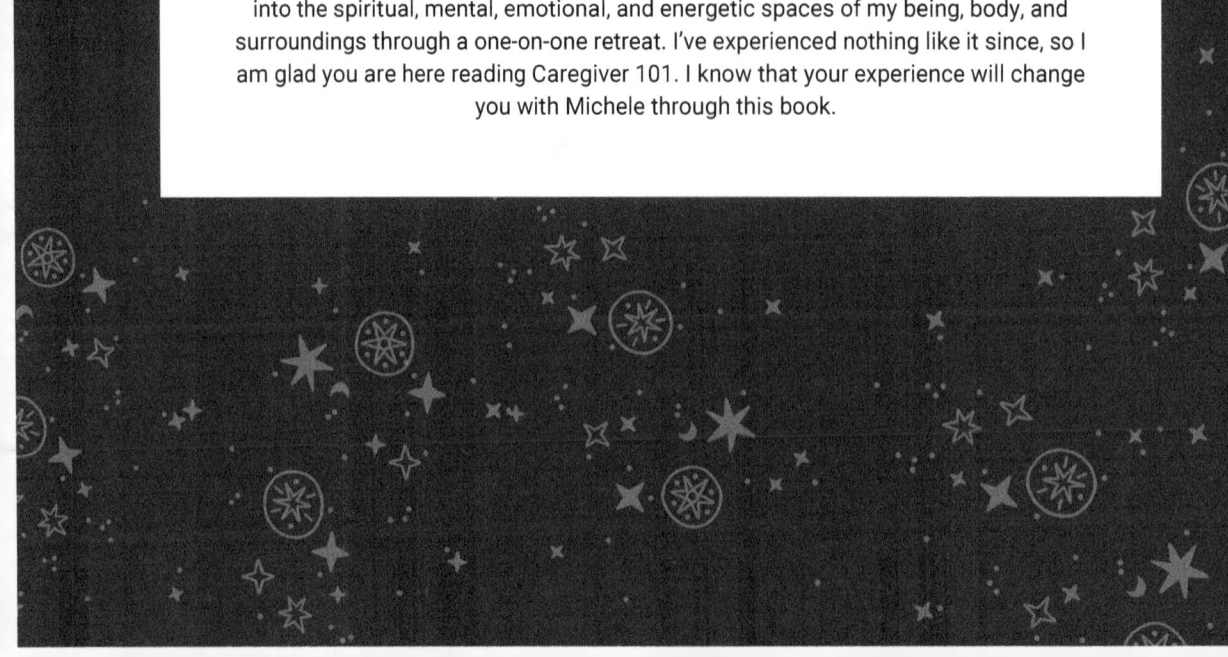

Testimonial

EMBRACE: *The 7 Stages of Grief Alignment* is created for every griefer; everyone feeling unqualified for and overwhelmed by the legal proceedings of loss of life, for those of us who are suffering alone because we can't bring ourselves to speak our emotional pain out loud to someone just yet or because you are keeping the pending end-of-life secret at the request of your loved one; for everyone cycling between the pain of anticipating a loss of precious life to needing to "hold it together" for your "normal" life and responsibilities to becoming angry and resentful back to pain again; and for every caregiver who needs care.

My favorite part about Michele's *7 Stages of Grief* is how she provides practical hope, by which I mean she has found the natural places where hope lives, bringing those places to light in this book. Michele is masterful at navigating the abundance of resources available to the caregiver and leads you to the path of help that is pragmatic and accessible. Michele is intimately aware of the caregiver's life because she gracefully helped her teenage son Nicky transition and was surrounded by much love.

My work with Michele has caused a seismic shift in my perspective and has improved my relationships with myself, my family, and the people who meet me. I am moved with infinite gratitude at the positive and priceless impact my work with Michele has had on my experience of motherhood and the beautiful relationship my daughter and I get to have. Now, I enjoy expanding my connection as she has become a selfless friend and true mentor.

I invite you to let this book change you for the better. Let this book support you and be there for you daily, especially when needed. Let this book be your guide. I want to leave you with this: Everything Michele has done since Nicky's return to Source has been a love letter to Nicky and a tribute to the permanent imprint of love and purpose he left with her. Ultimately, Michele hopes you may find your purpose and let it propel you through the rest of your precious life.

DISCLAIMER

All content within the 7 Stages of Grief Alignment Workbook is original and intended solely to promote mind, body, and spirit well-being. This material does not replace the expertise or advice of a licensed mental health professional. Grief experiences are unique to each individual, and while the workbook provides supportive tools and perspectives, it does not guarantee specific outcomes. If you are experiencing intense or extreme distress, please consult a professional.

By using this course, you acknowledge and accept these terms and conditions. The 7 Stages of Grief certification program, conceived and developed by Dr. Michele Bell, offers an innovative, holistic, and empathy-driven approach to understanding and navigating grief. It is rooted in comprehensive research and deep insight into the human experience of loss and recovery.

Program Overview:
- Embracing Growth in Grief: Recognize the transformative potential within grief.
- The 7 Stages of Grief: Explore the intricate emotional journey of grief, encompassing its multifaceted seven stages.
- Pivoting with Purpose: Equip yourself with practical tools to channel grief's raw energy into purposeful action.
- Understanding the Power of Resistance: Gain insights into the obstacles resistance can pose on the healing journey and learn strategies to address and overcome it.
- Coping Modalities: Discover and apply various coping methods tailored to individual grief journeys or to assist others on this path.
- Certification: As a culmination, the program offers a certification examination to ensure a comprehensive understanding of the 7 Stages of Grief methodology.

Engage with the 7 Stages of Grief, All-In-One Master Compilation program to acquire a compassionate and informed approach to navigating the intricate labyrinth of grief, whether for personal growth or as a professional commitment.

> Remember, every voice matters in bringing light to the shadows of grief. By uniting, we can raise awareness and create a world where everyone feels understood and supported during their moments of profound loss. I deeply appreciate your commitment to this cause. Please take a moment to sign the **Loss Awareness Day** petition on **Change.org**, inspired by the heartfelt endeavors of Lisa Marie Presley. Together, we can make a difference.
> With heartfelt gratitude and hope,
> MiMi

www.ingramcontent.com/pod-product-compliance
Lightning Source LLC
Chambersburg PA
CBHW061803290426
44109CB00031B/2929